High-Low-Split Poker

Seven-Card Stud and Omaha Eight-or-Better

for Advanced Players

By
Ray Zee

A product of Two Plus Two Publishing
www.twoplustwo.com

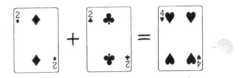

SECOND EDITION

SECOND PRINTING
OCTOBER 2002

Printing and Binding
Creel Printing Co.
Las Vegas, Nevada

Printed in the United States of America

High-Low-Split Poker
Seven-Card Stud and Omaha Eight or Better
for Advanced Players

For information contact:
Two Plus Two Publishing LLC
226 Garfield Drive
Henderson, NV 89014
(702) 896-1326
www.twoplustwo.com

For Linda K. Christensen

Table of Contents

Foreword

by Mason Malmuth

Rarely is a poker book written by one of the world's best players, but such is the case with this work. Ray Zee has been playing high-stakes poker against the top players in the world for more than twenty-five years and has achieved phenomenal success. In fact, whenever world-class players have been rated, Ray Zee has always been among the top ten.

Until recently, Ray kept a low profile, and he is not well known to the general poker-playing population. But to those people who have regularly played against him in some of the biggest games in the world, he is someone to fear. One well-known poker writer called him a "devastating money winner."

In the past, Ray shared his advice with only a small group of friends. In fact, a great deal of what I have put into print are ideas and concepts that I learned from this highly accomplished gambler. Put another way, whenever Ray shares his advice, it is well worth heeding.

Unlike the other three books in the *For Advanced Players* series, this text is actually two books in one. I consider this work as books three and four in the progression for two reasons.[1] First, many of the concepts applicable to seven-card stud eight-or-better are similar to those for Omaha eight-or-better. And second,

---

[1] The first two books in the series are *Hold 'em Poker For Advanced Players* by David Sklansky and Mason Malmuth, and *Seven-Card Stud For Advanced Players* by David Sklansky, Mason Malmuth, and Ray Zee, with the last book being *Tournament Poker For Advanced Players* by David Sklansky.

players mastering one game easily can make a transition to the other game.

Neither seven-card stud eight-or-better nor Omaha eight-or-better is a simple game. Consequently, only a small number of people are able to play these games at an expert level. But as Ray would be the first to advise, you do not become a professional overnight.

The writing of this text should help to promote eight-or-better, so more opportunities will be available for the poker expert of the future. These games are worth playing; they can be fun and very rewarding. But to be successful, you must be able to play very well.

There is some redundancy between the two texts. This was done for your benefit so that if you are interested in studying only one of the games, it will be easy to do. Of course, you are not expected to become an expert at both forms of poker that Ray Zee discusses, and I recognize that most of you will concentrate only on one game at a time. However, I believe this is a great opportunity to become proficient in two additional games.

As the representative of Two Plus Two Publishing, I consider it an honor to have been involved in this project. Working on this book has been not only exciting, but also a great learning experience for me. I'm sure it will be the same for you.

About Ray Zee

Ray Zee was born and raised in New Jersey, and spent his college years in the East as well. Unlike other students, Ray did more than just study. He began to gamble on the side in school, and when he graduated he was ready to start his career, which just happened to be in the dessert of Nevada.

Ray quickly realized that there were many opportunities in various forms of gambling and began to search for ways to exploit the inequities in many of the games. This included blackjack, horse racing, sports betting, slot jackpots, and of course his favorite game, poker.

It wasn't long before he became known as one of the top poker players and most knowledgeable gamblers in the world. And when we say world, we mean it literally because there are very few places where gambling is offered that Ray has not visited. In fact, you can go to many cardrooms all over the world, mention the name Ray Zee, and get an immediate response.

Ray usually chooses to play in very high stakes cash games, many of which feature some of the best players in the world. It has been said that "He leaves them with their eyes wide open when he departs." Ray is also one of the very few players that is considered expert in virtually every form of poker played for serious money. He is also one of the very few gamblers (still around) that attended the World Series of Poker Tournaments at Binion's Horseshoe Hotel and Casino in Las Vegas during all of its early years.

Rays book, *High-Low-Split Poker for Advanced Players* is recognized as the premier book on split pot games, and this has increased his following and helped to promote these games as well. He is considered an invaluable member of the Two Plus Two Publishing team, and his advice and wisdom is widely sought by many of his peers and adversaries at the gaming tables.

A Quick Note

Putting this text together was not easy. It took a lot of work, a lot of thinking, and a lot of perseverance. It also took a great deal of help from Mason Malmuth, whom I wish to thank in this space.

First, I want to express my appreciation to Mason for helping me organize, prepare, and present the text. Mason spent many hours reviewing this work, and his comments and suggestions are greatly appreciated. Second, I want to express my appreciation to Lynne Loomis for her work in editing this manuscript. Thanks to her expertise, you will be able not only to read this book, but to understand it as well.

I also want to thank David Sklansky for the use of some of the material that appears in the "Other Skills" section of each book. This material, which is presented in all the books in the *For Advanced Players* series, is a rewrite of the psychology and reading hands chapters from his book *The Theory of Poker*, with appropriate examples added.

This book contains a great deal of poker jargon. If you are not accustomed to the way I talk about poker in Nevada (and in other places where major poker rooms are located), the glossary at the end of this book should help you understand everything that is written. Those of you who are not familiar with many of the standard poker terms may want to read the glossary first.

Finally, I recommend that you read the chapter on high-low-split poker that is in Doyle Brunson's book *Super/System*. Even though this chapter does not target eight-or-better, many concepts and important ideas associated with all high-low-split games are discussed.

RAY ZEE

High-Low-Split Poker

Seven-Card Stud Eight-or-Better

For Advanced Players

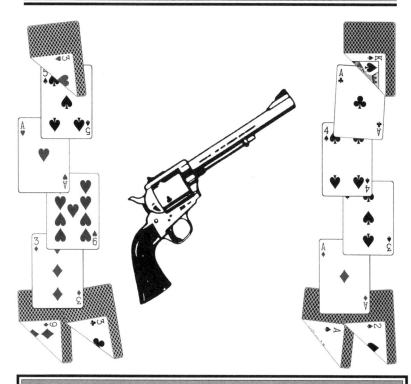

SEVEN-CARD STUD EIGHT-OR-BETTER FOR ADVANCED PLAYERS

Introduction

Seven-card stud eight-or-better is a fast game with numerous bets and raises. While skill is extremely important, luck can be a great equalizer on any given day. If you like to splash a lot of chips around, eight-or-better should be for you.

In this book, I will be talking about a game that is usually fairly tight, as most eight-or-better stud games are played at the medium and high stakes. At the lower stakes, the games tend to be much looser. However, since this is seven-card stud eight-or-better, there are not many playable hands, and it is hard to find a game that is too loose — unless it is an extremely low-limit one, which we will not be addressing. Remember, this text is for advanced players.

A lot of the value in eight-or-better, though it happens infrequently, is making a concealed high hand that appears to be low and thus enables you to punish some other high hands. One of the requisite skills for accomplishing this is the ability to read the cards correctly so you can identify the high hands. If it looks as though you have made the lock low, but you actually hold an ace-high flush, which is the lock high, then you are in one of the best situations this game offers.

In seven-card stud eight-or-better, the pot keeps building in a way that is slightly similar to a pot-limit game. In the later rounds, many raises often go in — that is, the betting action sometimes increases dramatically toward the end of the hand, especially in multiway pots.

In most other games, someone will bet and one or more persons usually will just call. But in stud eight-or-better, particularly when the pots are multiway — which is often the case — someone may have a lock for one side. This means that there are frequently two or more bets on some of the later streets, so in general, the implied odds are greater early in the hand. This increases the value of the right kind of hand, such as a small three straight which does better multiway.

When it looks as though you have the best hand, you almost always should bet or raise. Seven-card stud eight-or-better is not a game where you should attempt to trick your opponents by slow-playing or trying for a check-raise. Many of your adversaries will be scared of the best possible hand, and they will check along with you. Consequently, you need to bet your hands, or you will be a caller who doesn't win very much on his good hands but pays off when he is beat.

Exactly how you play your hand often determines whether you win or lose in the long run. Starting better than the other players helps enormously, as it does in any game, but most of your opponents also will "start good."

The weaker players will play too many second- and third-best hands — both high and low — but the better players will be in there with legitimate hands all the time. So you won't be outplaying most of your opponents by having better starting hands, but you might get an edge by making sure that your hands are more live than theirs.

Much of your advantage will come from correctly folding on fourth and fifth streets in spots where your opponents won't, and from jamming the pot at the right time when many other players don't. You also will make money by squeezing players out of pots and sometimes by stealing half of a pot that you were not supposed to get.

Finally, some players whom I have played against over the years in the higher stakes games, and whom you eventually may have the opportunity to play against, are Ken Flaton — one of the finest seven-card stud eight-or-better players; "Lefty" — a fine non-professional whose alertness at the table you would like to emulate; Dan Harrington — a great all-around player whom you could encounter in any game; David Sklansky — poker's top theorist; Frank Thompson — a real champ at this game; Jo-Jo — an energetic East Coast player; Tom Hufnagle — whom you will find at both this game and the Omaha split tables; Steve "Z" —

who loves all high-stakes games; Erik Seidel — a great New York tournament player; Norm Berliner — a top player; and Shirley from California — one of the regular women players.

Using This Book

This book will require you to do a lot of thinking. I recommend that the whole text be read first, then you can return to those sections that require more study.

Keep in mind that this book is for advanced players. If you are new to stud eight-or-better, it is best to play more conservatively than what is recommended. As you gain experience, you will begin to see where it is appropriate to try out all the plays that I discuss.

I also advise that you not jump right into a high-limit game. Even though the strategies in this book will win their share at the higher limits, especially if the opposition is not too tough, it is still better to start small and work your way up. In a game as complex as seven-card stud eight-or-better, there is no substitute for experience.

In addition, it is very important — as it is in all split games — to recognize when you have the best hand. This can be difficult at times, and a common beginner's mistake is to play a hand that appears to be good but is not really worthwhile. You should pay strict attention to when hands are playable and when they are not, especially on the later streets. Failing to do so is a costly error that an inexperienced player can easily make at this form of poker.

This section of *High-Low-Split Poker* wasn't written with a specific limit in mind, because seven-card stud eight-or-better does not get spread as much as some of the other standard poker games. But it frequently is played in the bigger cardrooms and is a mainstay in the side action of the major poker tournaments. The game is structured identically to standard seven-card stud. That is, a specific bet is permitted on third and fourth streets, and a double-sized bet is allowed on fifth, sixth, and seventh streets.

Note that in the text, hole cards are indicated with an underline. Otherwise the cards are face up. For example, if you

7

see A♣A♠A♥, the hand under discussion is three aces, and the two black aces are face down.

Incidentally, every serious stud player should read *Seven-Card Stud For Advanced Players*, co-written by David Sklansky, Mason Malmuth, and myself. Seven-card stud is the essential foundation for stud eight-or-better, and without a full understanding of basic stud, the eight-or-better version will be difficult to learn properly.

Finally, I also recommend that you read *The Theory of Poker* by David Sklansky, which covers many of the general concepts essential to beating seven-card stud eight-or-better. In fact, fully comprehending the more specific stud eight-or-better ideas presented in this book will be facilitated by first reading *The Theory of Poker*.

Why Play
Stud Eight-or-Better?

Of all the standard poker games, seven-card stud eight-or-better probably offers the most action. Numerous bets and raises, especially on the later betting rounds, make this game quite exciting, and the last card can change things dramatically.

But this doesn't mean that stud eight-or-better is a game of luck. Although you will go through some big swings and will see many pots going to live players, you also will have the opportunity to occasionally win some of the biggest pots in limit poker. And it is your skillful play that will make these pots so large. A weaker player dealt the same hand as you won't do nearly as well.

As noted, seven-card stud eight-or-better is not spread as much as the other standard forms of poker. Many cardrooms don't even offer it. However, there is an important exception: The game is played at almost every large poker tournament. For some reason, stud eight-or-better seems to flourish in this environment, and without a doubt it consistently produces some of the best poker games available at major events. Many players who seldom play this game will sit down during big tournaments, and the expert can do exceedingly well against them in the long run.

There is a lot of short-term luck in seven-card stud, and many stud players refer to their game as a "roller coaster ride." Well, seven-card stud eight-or-better is also a roller coaster ride — one that can go at very high speeds.

However, this game offers the opportunity for many expert plays, which may enable you to win half the pot as opposed to getting scooped, and sometimes will help you hog everything. The expert is able to pull off these plays because he sometimes can represent a hand very different from the one he actually holds.

10 Why Play Stud Eight-or-Better?

The result is that seven-card stud eight-or-better can be a rewarding game, though at times, it also can be frustrating. It's often difficult to find a game, but a few big cardrooms still offer stud eight-or-better fairly regularly, and as mentioned, there are many opportunities at the major tournaments — especially if you play at the higher limits. So if you become an expert at this game, expect to do very well. But remember that you won't become a champion overnight. It takes lots of study and playing experience.

Part One

Third Street

Third Street

Introduction

The most important decision in seven-card stud — both straight high and high-low split eight-or-better — is whether or not to play your hand on third street. But since stud eight-or better is spread mostly at the higher limits, the majority of your opponents will do a reasonably good job of hand selection. Moreover, most of the money in large pots goes in on the later betting rounds in stud eight-or-better, whereas in high-only stud, the large pots generally are built early in the hand.

Because of these factors, becoming a consistent winner in stud eight-or better requires that you play well on *every* street. Nevertheless, playing well begins with hand selection, so the information that follows is extremely important.

Starting Hands

Stud eight-or-better starting hands can be grouped into several categories according to how strong they normally are. Of course, this can change depending on your position, who has acted before you, the action up to that point, and so forth. But in general, the starting hand categories are ranked as follows:

Categories No. 1 and No. 2: Rolled-up trips and three cards to a low straight flush. These are the two best starting hands in seven-card stud eight-or-better. Rolled-up trips are discussed later in this section under a separate heading titled "Starting With Three of a Kind Wired." Three cards to a low straight flush is played like three small cards to a straight, which is covered in Category No. 4. However, keep in mind that the hand with flush possibilities is much stronger.

Category No. 3: Two aces with a low card. This holding is generally the third best starting hand in stud eight-or-better — even in multiway pots. However, aces do best in heads-up pots, which means that when you are dealt this hand, you usually should raise or reraise to thin out the field.

Categories No. 4 and No. 5: Three small cards to a straight and two small cards with an ace. The value of these two different hands runs fairly close. In a heads-up situation, despite what many people think, both hands are inferior to a high hand — unless it is obvious what the high hand is. If the high hand is disguised, the player holding it will be able to outplay his opponent and win the larger share of the pots. Remember, we are talking about an advanced player. A weak player holding the high hand often will not know where he stands, which will allow the low hand to outplay him. He will be made to fold when he shouldn't and will call to the end those times when he is likely to get scooped.

Many of your opponents will put a great deal of emphasis on three low cards to a straight. These hands are very strong and they do scoop a lot of pots. However, they do best in multiway pots when the cards needed to fill the open ends are very live and when these hands are not up against many other low hands.

So three low cards to a straight and two low cards with an ace are two of the best starting hands, and you frequently should play them strongly — and gamble with them — as long as your low cards are live. If some of your low cards are dead, then you should play these hands cautiously and be prepared to fold on fourth street if you catch bad and it appears that some of your opponents improve.

The reason these hands do well is that they not only win money when they make a low, but also make other hands — such as two pair, trips, straights, or flushes — that will beat some of the hands played for high. But these hands also bust out a fair amount of time, and not getting away from them quickly is one of the major mistakes that typical players make.

In addition, when playing one of these hands, you can get trapped by catching a rougher card than one of your opponents and discover that you are now against someone who is drawing better than you are. So in general, you want to have the smallest low hand to draw to; otherwise you will make the second-best low hand too often and will get punished.

Once there are four people in, three low cards to a straight, such as

does better than three low cards containing an ace that doesn't have straight possibilities, such as

Even though the latter hand makes two aces or aces up a lot of times, having straight potential frequently will allow you to bet your hand or to raise for value. Three low cards containing an ace won't get as much play, especially when you catch another ace — the game's premier scare card — which often slows the action.

When you start with three low straight cards and then catch an ace, you usually will have at least the best low draw and frequently a wheel draw. This will enable you to play with confidence, which translates into aggressive betting and raising.

In a heads-up situation, these two types of hands do about the same (although it is slightly better to hold two small cards and an ace). It depends on the player you are against and the live cards. An aggressive player will do better with the ace hand, and a passive player will do better with three low straight cards.

A surprisingly good hand against a small number of opponents is

If you are against a high hand, the 6♥7♠8♣ can escape for low as easily as

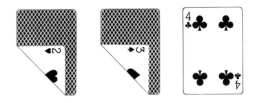

But it is also easier for the 6♥7♠8♣ to make a high hand. The winning high hand may be a medium pair or a hand like eights up — which might escape for high, especially if the pot is short-handed. One of the nice things about this hand is that it can be improved by two additional fourth-street cards that cause most other three-card low hands to bust out. Note that the 2♥3♠4♣ needs an eight or lower on fourth street, whereas the 6♥7♠8♣ can use a ten or lower.

Category No. 6: The best high hand on board. The best high hand out is another good starting hand. An example would be two kings or two queens, providing that this is the best pair. Holding an ace with either of these hands makes them even better, although having an ace is not necessary.

When playing what you think is the best high hand, it is very important that your cards are "live." Too often, low hands turn into two small pair. So a high hand going against one or more low hands must be very live to reduce the chances that it gets beat by two small pair.

Obviously, if you hold two aces and a high card, you probably have the best high starting hand. In this case, you would prefer to have one of the aces up. This is because when one ace is showing, your opponents likely will figure you for a low hand, which may allow you to win the pot on a later round if you catch more threatening low cards.

One idea that can't be overemphasized is to *throw away the second-best high hand*. The only possible exception is when you have a two-card low as well. If you have a high pair and think you might be up against a bigger pair, throw your hand away. If a king raises, discard two queens. If there are several overcards left to act, throw your big pair away.

Another time that big pairs can be costly is when several players with low cards showing have already entered the pot. You don't want to play against a low hand that has half the pot locked up and also has a draw at the high side. This is likely to happen when many low cards stay in. In addition, if someone catches an ace, you might not have the highest pair anymore. Thus big pairs are only marginally playable against a lot of low cards calling. Also, if an ace raises, you should throw your high pair away, even if there is a reasonable chance that the raiser has a low hand.

You would like to play two kings heads up against a player with a nine through a queen up. If you are heads up against someone with a deuce through an eight showing, that's still good but not as good as the other situation. You don't mind playing two kings against two opponents, as long as neither has an ace up. In most other spots, high pairs can be tricky to play. Advanced players can sometimes still play these hands, and limping in from a late position is an option to see what happens on fourth street. But if you lack experience, throwing high pairs away in other situations may save you a lot of bets. If you are trying to determine whether to play a big pair and the situation is close, here are some things to consider:

1. Is your hand live?
2. Do you have a two straight and/or a two flush?
3. Do you have a chance to make a low hand — that is, do you have a small card for a kicker?

But even a yes answer to all three questions does not necessarily mean that you should play.

Category No. 7: Three high cards to a consecutive straight flush. As long as your cards are live, these are some of the better starting hands. You can play these hands against several low hands, and you can take cards off. When you catch blanks, you usually can go to fifth or sixth street — unless there is a great deal of jamming — as long as your opponents' boards do not look too threatening.

Even though you may get jammed, especially if some of the hands that you are up against look scary, three high cards to a straight flush does show a profit. Sometimes when you are dealt one of these hands, your intuition will tell you not to get involved. But rest assured that they are worth playing as long as most of your cards are live.

Categories No. 8 and No. 9: Small pairs with an ace kicker and small pairs with a low kicker. Although both of these hands are extremely dangerous, having an ace kicker is preferable to having a small kicker. You frequently can see another card with a small pair and an ace kicker, as long as it does not cost more than a bet.

If you occasionally play these hands, keep in mind that they are very marginal. A small pair with a small kicker becomes worth playing only when it appears that no one has a strong hand. Moreover, you would prefer that the side card to your pair be a straight flush card. For example,

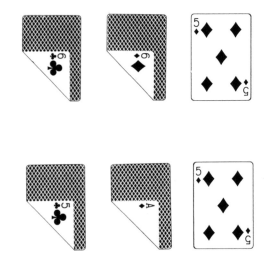

and

have more possibilities, especially if a low flush card comes. In this situation, you might make a lock for low and punish one or more high hands if you get lucky and also make a flush.

Most players will play small-pair, small-kicker starting hands. They are hard to throw away because they look good. However, you shouldn't play these hands unless the situation appears advantageous.

It is also slightly better for your pair to be at least sixes, because it is less likely that an opponent going for low will "accidently" make a pair and beat you. However, if one of your opponents has a high pair, whether your pair is sixes or something smaller won't matter. If you think you are up against a big pair, throw your hand away for a raise, especially if several players are already in the pot. But if you can get in for just a limp, you might want to take a card off. Keep in mind that you prefer to play this hand heads up against a player whose upcard is lower than the rank of your pair.

Also, if you do play one of these hands, you would prefer that your opponent's cards are not completely live and that your cards are very live. (See *Seven-Card Stud For Advanced Players* for a fuller explanation of this concept.) This is because your biggest value on fourth street is to make trips, a pair and a three straight, or a pair and three to a low flush. Your hand gains added value when it is more difficult for other players to improve.

When you play one of these holdings, remember that it's the type of hand that requires you to see fourth street cheaply. You usually will not play these hands in raised pots and in pots where there are scare cards behind you. For example, when the low card brings it in and there are other low cards or aces behind you, throw small pairs away.

Category No. 10: The razz hands. A hand like

is the type of hand that mediocre players lose a lot of money with. Notice that this hand not only is rough but also has neither straight nor flush potential. Hands like the 2♦6♥7♣ frequently should be discarded, especially for a raise in very high ante games and particularly when there is a high and another low out. This hand has very little equity, and it theoretically will lose money on all rounds of betting.

Even if you find yourself low on fourth street and the other low players have busted out, you frequently will still have trouble making the correct play and betting decisions on the later streets. Three unrelated low cards, whether played heads up or multiway, are big trouble, and the fair to intermediate players constantly get stuck with these hands.

If your razz hand is a little better than the example given, it becomes playable as long as it does not cost too much (no more than one full bet) and your cards are live. For example, if your hand is

you usually can play for one bet but not for two. However, if the cards you need to catch are dead, don't play for even one bet.

Category No. 11: Three low cards to an eight. This holding is not playable unless it has straight possibilities or includes an ace. Then it plays well only if it is the sole low hand working or if you are heads up against a probable weak hand.

Category No. 12: Three flushes. Since a lot of pots are split and it is tough to make a flush, for your three flush to be playable, you have to be in a multiway pot with several hands against you that look as though they are going high, or you must have two low cards. Also, your flush cards need to be extremely live.

In other words, discard most of your three flushes if there are two of your suit out. One of your suit on board is OK if you have a hand like

and it is cheap to enter the pot. But if several low cards are showing strength, throw these hands away. If you should catch high cards on the later streets, you will be in a situation where players will know that you are going for a flush or a high hand, and you will get jammed in by a high hand and a low hand. In short, you must make your flush quickly to survive this kind of situation.

Summing up, three flushes tend to do poorly in stud eight-or-better unless you have two low cards, and then your hand must be very live. Also, when you hold two low flush cards, it is always best to have one of them up so you are disguised as a low hand and perhaps can drive out a low hand later in the deal. Should you make both a flush draw and a low draw, you might be able to knock out the low hand and play only against the high hand or to knock out the high hand, just play against the low hand, and win the high half with almost nothing.

Category No. 13: Higher three straights. These hands do very poorly, but there are a few people who play them. When you are against these players, they are not as likely to have a high pair when they show a high card. Moreover, when higher three straights develop, they turn into strong and jamming type hands.

Category No. 14: Small pairs with a medium or large kicker. You should not play small pairs with a medium or large kicker unless most everyone has gone out, you are in a steal position, and you have a good chance to pick up the antes and bring-in.

Category No. 15: Medium high straights. Hands such as

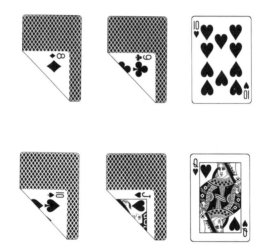

and

should just about never be played unless you are heads up against a weaker high hand or in certain situations where your cards are completely live, you are against several weak players, and no one has raised or is likely to raise. However, in general, these are trash hands and should be thrown away. Notice that even if two of your cards are straight flush cards — as in the second example — these hands still should be discarded.

Medium high straight draws against multiple low hands do even worse. Your opponents will know that you are going high and can severely punish you, plus many times you don't even make a pair to have a chance for the high end.

Final note: Even though the information provided is accurate, it is not absolute, since many starting hands are close to each other in value. The situation you find yourself in is often more important than the specific hand you are holding. Because a lot of hands run very close — such as the best high hand against a quality low hand — it is important to fully assess the situation before deciding on the strength of your starting hand. Some of these rankings can change dramatically depending on the particular three cards that you are holding and on the exact number of opponents that you are against.

In addition, it is very important to be playing the best hand, and not the second-best hand. In high-only seven-card stud, you often can play the second-best hand, such as a small pair with an overcard kicker, and chase. But in eight-or-better, this is normally not the case. Second-best hands do very poorly in this game, partly because you frequently do not know where you stand even when you improve. This is especially true in a multiway pot, as a lot of concealed hands — like trips, straights, and flushes — will appear on the river.

Finally, how to play your starting hand may not always be clear — that is, should you raise or just call? In general, you raise on third street only if you have a hand that plays better heads up, or if you have a hand that is very strong and several people are already in. If you have a typical playable three-card low and many players remain to act, you probably should just "limp in"; if other players already have called, you should call also. If there has been a raise in front of you, you generally should still call, but you usually should not call a double raise. The exception to just calling is when you are first in from a late position. Now you should raise, because you have the added equity of possibly being able to steal the antes.

Three of a Kind Wired

Occasionally you will be fortunate enough to be dealt rolled-up trips, one of the two best starting hands in seven-card stud eight-or-better. If your trips are high and it appears as though a lot of players will be in the pot, you might as well play your hand fast, stay right to the end, and see what happens. You should try to build as big a pot as you can.

It doesn't much matter whether you are heads up or in a multiway pot. When against only one opponent, you get to scoop more often. Against many opponents, a low usually will be made and sometimes you will get scooped; however, you generally will split and occasionally will even scoop a big pot.

When your high trips are queens or kings, it will look as though you have only a big pair and are raising just to limit the field. Thus the low hands will play very hard against you.

When your trips are between eights and jacks, you might want to play a bit easier so you can trap one or more high hands and then attempt to punish everyone on a later street. If you play these hands fast at first, it will look as if you are rolled up, and your opponents will realize that you probably have either aces in the hole or three of a kind.

When your trips are small, you have one of the best starting hands because it can be very deceptive. The best situation with a small set is to be against two high hands and not against low hands. If your hand appears to develop low, you can push it hard and jam the high hands.

Of course, if you have three wired aces, you have a dream hand. If your opponents will play with you, build a giant pot. But you need to slow-play three aces if you think you may drive out the high hands and get stuck playing against just the low hands.

Disguising Your Hand

When you play against players who obviously have hands roughly equal to yours and you seldom raise, you will be giving away too much information. Notice that you divulge something about your play by inaction as well as by action. When you do raise, your opponents will be able to put you on a big low hand or a high hand. So you have to do some raising or reraising when the hands appear roughly equal; otherwise you will be giving up too much of your deception. When your opponents have some doubt as to exactly what you hold, they may play improperly against you.

A lot of bets are almost automatic according to how the cards fall. By disguising your hand and thus encouraging some of your opponents to play badly, you will have them making automatic bets that are incorrect. So as you can see, it's to your advantage for someone to think you have something other than what you really have.

Disguising your hand doesn't always mean that you make your opponents think you are going high when you are going low, or vice versa. A lot of times you might make them think you have a made low hand when you actually have only four low cards and a pair. This type of play may encourage another low draw or a made low (but one that is not very good) to fold. In addition, it might allow you to value bet two pair on the end into a hand that looks like only a high pair.

By disguising your hand, you will make it difficult — if not impossible — for your opponents to correctly ascertain the exact strength of your holding. If you are successful in doing this, you will get them to make some major errors against you.

Ante Stealing

Ante stealing in seven-card stud eight-or-better is fairly straightforward. It's not as important in this game as it is in many other forms of poker, because advantageous opportunities come up less often. But in the right spots, ante stealing still has value. As a word of caution, though, don't attempt this play with two or more low cards behind you, since many players like to call with low cards.

It is easiest to steal when you have an ace up, because an ace — the premier scare card in almost every game — is even stronger in eight-or-better. Another good hand to steal with is a high card when there are one or two cards ranking nine or higher that still remain to act. Most players, even good ones, will now fold medium pairs, because they are afraid to play against a possible big pair.

If you are going to try to steal into low cards, you need an ace up or a medium low card, such as a six, rather than a deuce or a trey. When you are showing a medium low card, there will be some doubt as to whether you hold a higher pair than your opponents might have. That is, your hand will be less defined, which means that it will be less likely that one of your remaining opponents will want to contest it.

Here's an example of a typical ante steal. Suppose you have a jack up, there are a queen and a nine behind you, and you raise. The player with the queen up usually will go out unless he has a pair of queens, in which case you will be reraised. In addition, he probably will throw away some other hands that he would have been interested in playing had you just folded or called. Assuming that the queen now folds, the player with the nine up generally will also fold, even if he has two nines. Since you raised into the queen, it won't look as though you are stealing. Because the game under discussion is seven-card stud eight-or-better, note that if this opponent had an eight showing instead of a nine and held a pair of eights, the result might be different.

Getting
Reraised on a Semi-Steal

Suppose you have a medium small pair with a small kicker, such as

Most everyone folds and you raise the low card, hoping to steal the antes or to play heads up with the bring-in. If you are in what appears to be a steal position, an aggressive player frequently will raise back with a low card that is smaller than your pair. In this case, you usually will have the best hand, and your opponent is probably raising on three small cards or a small pair with a bigger kicker (which could be an ace), trying either to knock you out or to better define your hand.

When this happens, you should raise back and play the hand aggressively as the leader, since it is unlikely that you are beat. You might be against a large pair in the hole, but if that is the case, you are not a huge underdog.

This play works extremely well because your hand is not clear to your opponent, plus you probably do have the best hand. If you catch a baby on fourth street and your opponent catches anything from a nine on up, you sometimes will win the pot right there, as he will now be afraid of what you may have.

If you catch bad and your opponent catches small, you will have to make a tough decision, which might be to throw your hand away. If you both catch small cards, you probably will still want to lead just for deception, but be cautious.

If you both catch bad, your hand becomes stronger. Your opponent likely will have a busted three low — in which case his hand is terrible — or a smaller pair than you have, and he won't know where he stands. If he plays, he probably is taking a card off in the hope that you have three low cards.

When an Ace Raises

When an ace raises, you should not play many hands. This includes high pairs, which usually should be thrown away since you can't take the chance that you are playing against a pair of aces. Even if your opponent holds three low cards, he still could catch another ace. When you do play against an ace, you'd better have three very good low cards. You don't want to have a high hand. This is most important against a tight opponent; it is also important, but to a lesser extent, against an action player.

If you have a big pair, such as two kings or two queens, and an ace is behind you, you should be leery of raising or even playing your hand. This is especially true if the ace is held by an aggressive player, who will tend to reraise you not only with aces, but also with an ace and two low cards or an ace and a small pair. He will assume that he can outplay you, because you won't know where you stand. Even if the aggressive player has the worst hand percentagewise, he may have the best of it moneywise.

So when there is an ace on board, you should be careful about entering the pot if that player is yet to act. If he has already raised, unless he is a maniac who raises all the time, you should be extremely cautious about playing. But even when playing against a maniac, keep in mind that he is starting with the best card in the deck.

When the Bring-In Raises

It doesn't happen often, but occasionally the bring-in — the player with the lowest card on board — will start the action with a raise. This always means that he has a playable hand, and it usually means that he has a fairly good hand but not a great hand.

When the bring-in raises, he typically holds three small flush cards, three small straight cards, or a high pair in the hole. Of these three possibilities, his most likely hand is a high pair in the hole, and he is trying to limit the field. The exception is when this player is steaming, which can be determined based on how he is conducting himself and how he has fared in the last few pots.

In this situation, you should play very tightly. Players likely to be contesting the bring-in will have quality hands. Also, you will not have the added equity of the bring-in money, since this player usually will not be folding because of additional raises.

Third Street

Afterthought

As will be seen in detail later in the text, it is important to disguise your hand where possible. Of course, you usually won't be able to do this. But when you can, it could make the difference between winning a small pot and a big pot. This, in turn, can help make the difference between being a winner rather than a loser in seven-card stud eight-or-better.

Also keep in mind how important an ace is. When someone enters the pot with an ace as an upcard, many hands that appear playable to an inexperienced player should be thrown away. In fact, an ace may be more important in this game than in any other standard form of poker.

Part Two

The Later Streets

The Later Streets

Introduction

To be successful in seven-card stud eight-or-better, it's imperative that you play very well on the later streets, as most of your opponents will not make too many errors on third street. That is, in most cases, they will start with good hands. You will, of course, occasionally run into a player who gives his money away by playing foolish hands on third street. But in general, you see few of these players — especially at the higher limits — and when you do come across one, he won't last very long.

You also must not be timid in this game. Stud eight-or-better is a game of jamming. Sixth street, and to a lesser degree all the other streets, can be very expensive. Sometimes it is correct for you to do the jamming, and it's critical that you recognize these situations and take maximum advantage of them. Also, you must be able to recognize when other players will begin jamming. This may mean that your hand, which looks good but not terrific, should hit the muck.

General Strategy

In stud eight-or-better, it is difficult to predict when the raising will start, because on the later streets, cards can come out that dramatically change hands. As an example, low draws can pick up flush potential.

Consequently, a reasonable strategy to pursue when the pot is still small — particularly on fifth street — is to get out any time that your hand does not appear to be the best hand for one way or the other. This is especially true if there are hands out that are well-defined in each direction. If you fail to fold in this situation, you may get trapped for a bigger bet and several raises on a later round. The only exception to folding is when you have a two-way hand. In this case, it is usually worth chasing slightly better one-way hands.

Needless to say, if no one catches anything that appears to make his hand better, you may want to go further with your hand. You also can go further if you are against players who tend not to jam unless they have a cinch hand. Against more aggressive players who jam a lot, you need to be careful about getting too involved in the pot.

When you hold a good hand, you should be a player who frequently jams. Your opponents will fear you, plus many players don't like to put a lot of money into the pot. So if you are a jamming type player, most opponents will be cautious when playing against you. They will check to you more, and you will be able to control the size of the pot and how you want to play your hand.

The fear factor is very important in this game (as it is in most games). You want your opponents to fear you not because you always have a good hand, but because your hand is difficult to read and you are willing to put a lot of money in the pot. (If your opponents always know you have a good hand, they will be able to define it and play accordingly.)

An extremely important skill is the ability to size up what it will cost you to see the hand through, since there are frequently many bets and raises on the later rounds. In other games, it is usually easy to figure out what the hand will cost to go all the way. But in this game, there can be many bets and raises, so you must have the ability to make a good estimate of how many more bets the hand is likely to cost.

Specifically, if you get into a spot where it looks as though you might get squeezed on a later round, be aware that this round might cost three or four bets instead of one. Hence, instead of paying two or three bets to go to the river, as you would in most other games, it can easily end up costing you seven to ten bets. This means that your implied odds can change dramatically. You might make a great deal of money if you draw out, but trying to do so may not be worth the price.

A related idea is that you can play further against players who don't jam much and are reluctant to try to squeeze you out. On the other hand, against very aggressive players who like to cap all the bets off, plus to raise and jam even in some of the more marginal situations, you will have to give up on your hand a lot sooner. When you get trapped against this type of player and you hold a second-best hand that needs to draw out, it can be suicide.

Consequently, it is very important to accurately judge your opponents by how they play their hands. Knowing whether some people play tight or loose is not enough. You also must know how fast they play and how often they jam the pot.

Against those players who play very fast, you want to play two-way hands, hands that are well-disguised, and the bigger hands, because you will make much more money than normal. Against players who are passive and conservative — and many players are this way — you can play a few more hands.

Following are a few general concepts for seven-card stud eight-or-better. Many of these ideas will be discussed in more detail later in the text, but a quick overview of them here should be most helpful.

Concept No. 1: One-way hands, especially heads up, go way down in value. Let's look at a simple calculation. Suppose on fifth street that there are two bets in the pot. You have a chance to win only half the pot, but you think it is likely that you will win that half. Is a call correct?

It turns out that calling in this situation may be wrong. Since going to the end will cost you three bets, which you will forfeit if you get scooped, you need to win your half of the pot at least 75 percent of the time for your calls to be correct. This is because you are risking three bets to win only one bet. Consequently, if you are not a big favorite to win your half of the pot, you should throw your hand away.

For example, suppose you hold

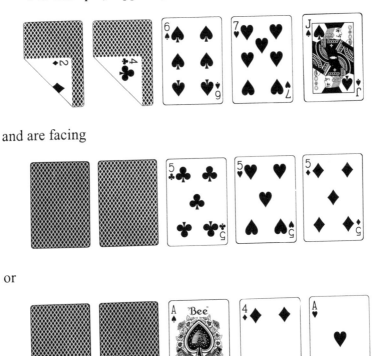

and are facing

or

Throw your hand away. The only exception is when the pot is large.

Here's another example. You hold

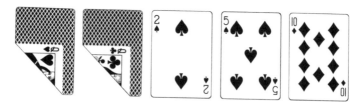

and are looking at a hand like

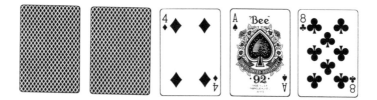

or

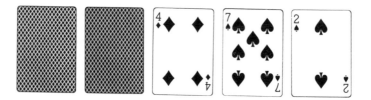

You may want to fold. But these examples are not as apparent as the previous examples, since you have a chance to scoop. And if your high hand doesn't win everything, it still might be good enough to win the high side. If your big pair were against

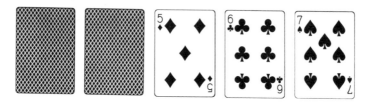

you would play on, as it is now unlikely that a straight or a bigger pair will be able to beat you.

Concept No. 2: One-way hands, where you must lose half the pot, are also risky played multiway. For example, in a three-way pot, you need to be a 2-to-1 favorite or better to win your side for a bet or raise to be correct. Whenever you bet into two people who call, you can win only half a bet. The opponent who wins the other side will get the other half-bet.

Here's an example. An opponent showing

bets, and his most likely hand is three queens. Another opponent calls with

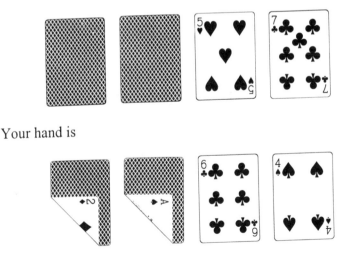

Your hand is

In this situation, you have only a call. Even though you are a favorite to win your side, you are not a 2-to-1 favorite. (There is an exception to just calling. If you are only a small favorite to win half the pot, but a bet or raise may cause your main opponent to fold, you should proceed accordingly. There is more discussion on this idea later in the text.)

Concept No. 3: In general, you should fold if it is still early in the hand and someone else is favored over you, no matter what the direction. If you are not a favorite to win at least one way and the pot is not yet large, usually throw your hand away.

But there are some exceptions. Suppose your hand is

and you are against an apparent high pair and what you perceive as an eight-high, four-card low. In this case, you have a good enough hand to take one more card.

You also can play marginal hands if they have a chance, even a small one, to win the whole pot. Here's an example. Suppose your first four cards are

If one of your opponents appears to have a high pair and your other opponent appears to have a better four-card low, you can keep playing. This is because you have a chance to scoop the whole pot, and if you don't scoop, you still might win either the high side or the low side.

This concept is why high hands are enormously better in seven-card stud eight-or-better than they are in regular high-low stud. In eight-or-better, high hands can win the whole pot, but without the qualifier for low, they usually can't do that. Nevertheless, many players — usually those without much experience — overrate the high hands, especially in full games.

Concept No. 4: If you can win only half the pot but have that side locked up, don't knock out other players. The reason for this should be obvious: You can't make any more money if the pot becomes heads up.

Concept No. 5: Try to eliminate your opponents if this will enable you to win the whole pot. This is more or less the opposite of Concept No. 4. In a multiway pot, if you have made a quality high hand, knocking out your opponents is often the correct strategy.

Here's an example. Suppose you have a big flush on fifth street. Your opponents show

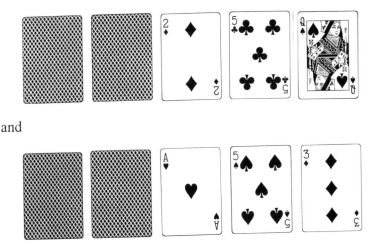

and

If the player holding the A♥ 5♠ 3♦ bets, you should raise in an attempt to get the other opponent going for low to fold. You actually lose a little if the original bettor already has a low made. But if he doesn't, your chances of scooping have been greatly increased, and your overall expectation has gone way up. You should make this play at every opportunity.

How Far Do You Go?

Although many hands may be similar in value, you cannot go as far with some of them — unless they quickly improve — as you can with others. Those hands that you normally take further should be played with more strength earlier, since you are more likely to go to the end and get your money back. Hands that you often fold early should be played in the opposite manner. That is, with these hands, you want to put in as little money as possible.

Specifically, a hand like three small straight cards, particularly if the cards are suited, can be taken a lot further into the hand. The same is true for two aces with a small card. If you catch a bad card, you generally can still take another card off even if the pot is raised, unless someone else's hand develops strongly.

But don't get married to these hands. For example, if you have aces with a small card and someone who raised with a high card up now pairs his door card, you should fold. You also should consider folding a small three straight that does not improve when someone who started with a small card up catches a suited baby on fourth street.

Fourth Street

In general, the biggest mistake you can make in stud eight-or-better is to call frequently on fourth street when you catch a bad card — especially if you are going low and your opponents catch a second good low card. This is because that second low card must help them in one way or another. (If it doesn't improve their lows, it pairs them.)

For instance, suppose you are high and a couple of your opponents catch another low card that is close in rank to their third-street cards. In this situation, you might be against more than one four straight, as well as a low draw. It is now time to fold your high hand. If you don't fold, you often will not know how to play your hand and will get jammed. However, if the pot is heads up, your opponent who appears to be going low catches a fourth-street card close in rank to his third-street card, and you hold a good high hand, you can take a card off.

Suppose you start with three low cards in a multiway pot, there is a high hand against you, and someone has raised with a wheel card up, showing early strength. This player then catches another small card close in rank to his door card, which means he could have a four-card straight. You also make a four-card low by catching a seven or an eight, which leaves you with what looks like the second-best low draw (and a rough one at that). Unless you also have a straight or flush draw, you almost always should go out.

Most players don't fold in this spot. They take off another card to see whether the other low hand will miss. This is wrong. The only time it is correct to play in this situation is when you are last to act, so you know you will not be raised.

If you are not last, the other players will be quick to raise, because they know you are drawing to only a rough low with virtually no chance of making a high hand. They will not be afraid to punish you.

Suppose you have a hand like

and an opponent has a hand like

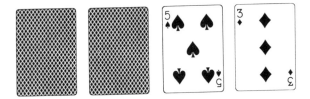

Notice that you have no straight draw. The high bets, and your opponent holding the low hand now raises. You must muck your hand, as you are going to be second-best in what easily could be a jammed pot.

If you are going to play this hand, you should reraise and try to knock out the high hand. (I don't recommend that you do this often.) Your reraise should scare the player with the high hand and may make him fold a hand like two queens. Now you'll get to play heads up against the other low hand and will have a better chance.

Still, it is best to throw these hands away in this situation. They are money losers, even if it is possible that you might have the best low hand. Remember, you have to call a raise, you are playing for only a small share of the pot, you don't know where you stand, and many of the cards left in the deck that the raiser can catch are very scary for you. A call in this situation is justified only if there is no raise.

Suppose you start with a small three straight and catch close to perfect. In this case, just go ahead and bet the hand for value. Usually most everyone will call, because:

1.   They won't know what you have,
2.   They will hope to catch up, or
3.   The pot will look bigger to them than it really is.

Don't get tricky. Play your hand straightforward. That is, bet it.

If you are playing for a high hand, and on fourth street your cards start to fall a bit dead, it is probably best to get out when you are looking at an opponent with two low cards. It is not that your hand has gone to a percentage loser, but that it is a playing loser. The player going low will be able to outplay you, you won't always know where you stand, and your hand will be tougher to improve.

If you catch a bad card on fourth street and are against two opponents who have both caught low straight cards to go along with their low third-street cards, you probably should get out, even if your cards are live. If one opponent caught good and the other caught bad, you might want to bet, raise, or check-raise and try to force the low hand that caught bad to fold. (However, if he is a decent player, he will fold anyway, so a call usually will be enough.) As long as it remains live, your hand should play reasonably well against one person with two low straight cards. You are in a scary situation, but your hand still has value.

When the player on fourth street who started with a low card now catches another low card, which is a straight flush card, it is usually best to go out. You will have to play the rest of the hand in the dark, because you won't know whether your opponent is going high or low. Unless you have improved a great deal or have a hand that can win on its own — which may not be likely at this point — you should fold unless the pot is quite large. Even though you might be throwing away the best hand, your fold is still correct, because it now will be extremely easy for your opponent to outplay you with two low cards to a straight flush showing.

The situation is often similar if your opponent catches a suited ace. That is, you usually should fold. In fact, the suited ace is frequently more dangerous, as in most cases, you will be behind in both directions.

Also, if you are playing the high hand and a player who stood a raise going in catches a live ace on fourth street, it is usually best to give up your hand if your opponent bets. Routinely calling in this spot will prove costly.

If you start with a low hand and catch bad, usually get out. The exceptions are:

1. The pot is extremely large.
2. You started with a premium hand. Or
3. Everyone catches bad.

For you to continue playing when you catch bad, one of these exceptions needs to be in force.

For example, if you start with a hand like

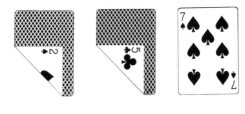

and catch the

usually give up. Calls in this situation prove to be very expensive in the long run.

Also on fourth street, think about how to set up your play of the hand. When it is heads up, the cards usually fall so that the best hand will be betting. The high hand either will lead or, if the low hand looks strong, will check and usually make "crying calls."

When many players are in the pot on fourth street, you will be able to determine how you want to play the hand and how you want it to develop. For instance, if you have a strong hand, you might want to play it fast, but you also may want to look weak and play it slow.

Generally, if a player who showed strength on third street catches good, he will be checked to and will bet. If he doesn't bet, most of the time that card was of no help. A few tricky players will check if they have made four to a very strong hand, but most players will just bet it and try to take the value.

If you have the best high hand, this is the time when you must decide whether to narrow the field and play against just one or two players. But if you don't think you can narrow the field, you don't want to take charge and put a lot of money in the pot.

It is sometimes good not to play fast so you can determine where the strength lies. (This is not the same as a slow-play.) By seeing where the strength is, you will be able to make better decisions later in the hand. Remember, this is a game where many hands run close in value, and you don't always have information as to what your opponents hold. Not playing fast may allow you to save money or to subsequently punish someone, since mistakes on the later rounds can be very costly, especially when drawing dead or close to it.

When you have the high hand, most everyone will know you are going high, so your play should be fairly straightforward. If your hand looks strong, you should be betting or raising with it; if it looks weak, you should be either folding or calling.

But when you have a quality low hand on fourth street or a hidden high hand, such as small trips or aces in the hole with two small cards, you might want to disguise your hand. That is, you may want to play it differently from what most people think is correct. By doing this, you may not get the optimal number of bets on fourth street. But later, when the big bets come, you will be much better off if some of your opponents are now misreading your hand. For instance, if you look low but actually have a strong high hand, you may get to knock a weak low out of the pot by jamming on a later street.

Check-Raising on Fourth and Fifth Streets

Check-raising is one of the key tools that an expert player will use on fourth street and, to a lesser extent, on fifth street. In many other games, check-raising doesn't come into play as much, because you can't always count on an opponent betting. But since hands are often disguised in eight-or-better, the check-raise can be used frequently.

Usually the player who is low and catches another low card will bet, or the high hand will bet if his opponent(s) busts out. Thus, you will be in situations where it is virtually certain that the attempt to check-raise will be successful. Of course, you should check-raise only with hands that merit doing so.

Giving a free card when trying to check-raise is not so terrible in seven-card stud eight-or-better, because most opponents will call your bet anyway (although they may not call for two bets). Consequently, if you give a free card, you generally cost yourself only a piece of the bet as opposed to the pot. Players don't often have hands where an off-the-wall card can make them a monster.

The check-raise will enable you not only to gain a double bet, but also to frequently knock out players who are going the same way as you are. Check-raising is very strong when you have a high hand, knock out another high hand, and get to play heads up against a low who doesn't have high possibilities and may bust out.

Here's an example. Suppose you have two aces but also have low possibilities developing. If your check-raise knocks out another high hand, or if you can knock out a low hand and play against a weaker high hand, where you have a chance to make a low if he should outdraw you for high, you have accomplished a lot.

As you can see, the check-raise is a valuable tool in seven-card stud eight-or-better, and few players use it enough. However, an advanced player will use the check-raise at every advantageous opportunity.

Fifth Street

Suppose on fourth street that you have a good four-card low, which is also a four straight or four flush, and you bust out on fifth street. If your hand is live and it appears that you still have a good chance to scoop, you should bet. Why? Because you might pair your bad card on sixth street, and it will look scary enough for you to bet again and possibly win the pot right then. So there can be an advantage to continue betting, even when it is not clear that you have the best hand.

Frequently, especially at the higher stakes, you will be contesting many pots heads up on fifth street. When this happens, you often will find yourself going in the opposite direction of your opponent. If you hold the high hand, you usually will be trying to knock out your opponent with the probable low hand. But the apparent low hand may actually be the best high hand, or a made low hand with a draw at a high hand, or four very good low cards with a pair. This makes your opponent a favorite over you, unless your high hand has also improved.

So you generally will be betting into the low hand, unless he has three low cards up. In that case, you want to be checking and calling, or checking and folding, depending on the three low cards — that is, what you think you might be up against — and on exactly how strong your high hand is.

If you are against a possible good four-card low (with one bad card), and you think you are also against a straight draw, you should be inclined to check, unless your hand is exceptionally strong. But if you think your opponent may have three low cards, a pair, and a bust card, then you should bet and be willing to call a raise if it comes.

You may find yourself in a three-handed pot on fifth street. Suppose it appears that one of your opponents is going the same way as you are, but the other opponent is going in the opposite direction. If you have the best hand, it is very important to try to eliminate the player going the other way, and you must play your hand in such a way as to make this possible. Should you be successful, you will get to play heads up with someone going your way when you have the best hand.

Eliminating the player going in the opposite direction can be difficult. It might take something tricky, such as giving a free card until sixth street and then raising. But sometimes the hands can be deceptive, and you might trick this opponent into thinking you have him beat.

Here's an example. Suppose you and another player are going low, and you wish to knock out your other opponent, who has a weak high. On fifth street, you have

Your opponent who appears to be going low is in the middle with

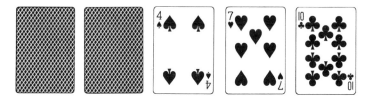

and the player going high has

If you check, the player in the middle probably will check behind you. When the player going high then bets, you should check-raise. Since it looks as though you may have made aces, the player in the middle might call the double bet, while the player on the end — who is going high — may fold. In the unlikely event that both of your opponents fold, that's even better.

Most players who hold four low cards and a bad card become concerned that they might get jammed in later and not make their low hand. If a player in this spot checks and calls, it is almost certain that he has a low draw but doesn't have a good straight or flush draw to go along with it. If he has an additional draw, he often will bet — especially an aggressive player — unless he is playing against some scary boards.

You also must mix up your play a fair amount on fifth street. For example, with a busted low hand and a high card, you may want to check-raise or even jam to disguise your hand. Even if you are taking a little the worst of it, an occasional play like this will confuse your opponents. At a later time, when you play disguised trips the same way, the good players won't know whether you have a high hand or a low hand.

If good players can put you on a high hand when you hold a hand that looks low, they will come with weaker low hands. Notice that this is exactly what you don't want. You want them out when you have a disguised high hand, as you prefer to play against only high hands. This is where (and why) you have to mix up your play enough so that good players can't read you. Otherwise, when those great situations come up and you have a disguised high hand, you won't be able to get out some of the weaker low draws. By the way, these great situations don't occur often, but when they do, they are very profitable.

Most players who make a low hand are in the pot till the end, unless an opponent's board looks very scary. Although few players are capable of laying down a made eight or a rough seven, the better players can throw away these hands when they are looking at something like

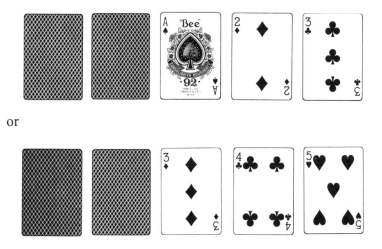

or

Incidentally, not throwing away rough made hands against strong boards is one of the major errors in this game. These calls aren't even correct in razz, where you are playing for the whole pot. But since many of your opponents are not experienced razz players, they will make this mistake.

As stated previously, high hands are good starting hands, but they become weak on fifth street when it is obvious that someone has made a low. The big advantage that you had with a high hand — namely, the potential to win the whole pot — is now gone. Thus, you must consider folding.

You will tend to play on if it is heads up and the pot is fairly large. You also should continue playing if it appears that you are not likely to get scooped. For example, if the obvious low hand has a board like

it will be very hard for him to make a straight. However, you should fold if you are looking at a hand like

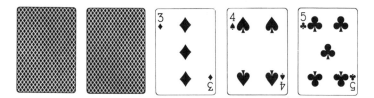

But when you have a big pair and your opponent's board is something in between these two examples, you should consider how live the possible straight or flush cards are for your opponent. For example, if your opponent's hand is

and several treys and fours are already dead, you should continue playing. On the other hand, if these cards are all still live, you probably should throw your big pair into the muck.

It also is always scary if an opponent's third low upcard is an ace. If he started with an ace, he now may have you beat for high. If he doesn't, he probably has made his low. In this situation, you usually should go out.

The high hands do well if the low hands have busted out by fifth street. This is the time to push high hands, since your opponent will have only two cards left to beat you.

By the way, if you have any doubt as to whether you should continue playing or fold on fifth street, you should fold unless you have a good chance for half the pot or a decent chance for all of it. If you have only a decent chance to win half the pot and you routinely keep playing, you can expect to go broke.

Sixth Street

In seven-card stud played straight high, it is uncommon to fold on sixth street. You only occasionally will see a pot where someone will throw his hand away with one card to come, unless either a very scary card hits or there is a bet and a raise before a third person can act. If you can call on fifth street, you usually can call on sixth street in the hope of improving on the river.

But in stud eight-or-better, just the opposite is true. That is, you frequently should fold on sixth street. This is because one or more of your opponents can catch a card that might mean you are drawing dead, plus there may be (at least) a bet and a raise. In this game, sixth street is frequently jammed in a multiway pot. (In high-only seven-card stud, there are fewer times when there is more than one bet on sixth street.)

Knowing when to lay down hands like two big pair on sixth street becomes crucial. In seven-card stud high, you normally do not give up these hands. You frequently draw — even if you think you are beat — because you generally get enough pot odds to make it worthwhile.

In seven-card stud eight-or-better, when there is a great deal of betting and raising on sixth street, the pot is virtually certain to be split. You will not be getting the odds you need to attempt to draw out on the high end when you have only two pair. Usually, the only time you should try to catch is when you have a lot of outs. Specifically, it is OK to call in those spots where you have a good low draw, a flush draw, or trips, and you are getting the proper odds.

Seventh Street

On seventh street, the situation frequently becomes scary. This is because everyone gets a downcard, and if you happened to have the best hand on sixth street, your opponents likely are drawing to beat you. (The last card generally has more impact in stud eight-or-better than in any other form of poker regularly spread in public cardrooms.) However, you usually need to bet anyway and see what happens.

The exception to betting is if you have a made low hand and are up against a high hand and one or more opponents who were drawing to a better low. If you bet, the high hand will raise, and the other low hands either will fold or will reraise if they have improved to what they were hoping for.

But if you have the best low hand and are against other players with made low hands who are likely to pay off whether they have improved or not, then you of course should bet or raise (into them). It is worth taking this chance.

If you have a high hand, there are low hands against you, and a split pot is certain (as long as one of the low hands hasn't improved to a straight, a flush, or something better, and it is likely that one or more of these draws is out), you should just check and call. In this case, you are hoping to split the pot, and if there is a bet and a call, you might even make money on seventh street.

However, you should lead on the end with your high hand if there are two or three players in the pot who look as though they will call with weaker high hands. Most players will check, because they are afraid of running into a low hand that has turned into a straight or a flush. But there is frequently value in betting.

Here is another situation that comes up on seventh street. You miss a low draw but make a pair, perhaps even a small pair. A player who has been betting most of the way bets again, and it appears that he has a low hand. Sometimes if he is bluffing, and if your pair beats a pair that he could have made on an earlier street, you may have the "hogger." If he does have the low, your (small) pair may enable you to split the pot.

Thus, you must keep in mind that if your low hand has busted out but you have a small pair, it still may be worth half the pot or perhaps even the whole pot. If there is plenty of money in the center, it is often worth a call and sometimes worth a raise when the low hand bets and you have missed. Your raise might even knock out the high hand who has only one big pair. Even though the opportunity for this play may come up a couple of times a night, you can't make it all the time. However, it is worth considering against the right opponent.

Suppose in a two-person pot that you have an obvious high hand, such as a pair of kings. On an earlier street, your opponent made three low cards on board, and you both checked. You now suspect that his most likely hand is four low cards with a pair.

Further suppose that on the river, you make kings up. Should you bet? Even though most players will check and call, because they are afraid that they might run into a straight, this is wrong. What normally happens is that if your opponent makes two pair, he will pay off your bet and you get to hog the whole pot. If he makes a low — which probably will be a cinch low — he will raise, you will call, and you will split the pot. You will lose only if he does make the straight or if he makes three of a kind. So frequently, betting is the answer. Even though there is much risk, this bet shows a profit in the long run.

In another case, suppose you have a big pair in the hole, and it looks as though you are against someone who also has a big pair. He has been calling you down, but his pair does not appear to be as large as yours, and you have some small cards up. If your opponent checks to you on the river, you want to bet your one pair against him, because he will call hoping to split the pot against a low hand.

In seven-card stud eight-or-better, when it appears that someone has a low hand, it becomes correct to call with almost any pair. But you never value-bet your big pairs in this spot. Similarly, if you are going for low and someone holding an obvious big pair checks to you, you should bet your hand for value. Since it looks as though you are betting a low, your opponent almost always will call with his one pair.

As you can see, there are many opportunities in stud eight-or-better for value bets on the end. In many games, especially tight games, a large part of your profit easily can come from these seventh-street bets.

This discussion on betting for value illustrates another important concept: You cannot bluff a high hand with any hand that looks as though you are going low. The only way you could get away with this is if you catch an ace along the way and come out betting or check-raising when you don't have the possible low made. For example, suppose you bust out on fourth street, catch an ace on fifth street, and then check-raise. Your opponent might think you have made aces, and this may enable you to bluff out a pair on the end, when actually you have made this play with four low cards.

However, there are a few situations where you should bet as a bluff. As an example, suppose you have

and are against one opponent who shows

Notice that you are beat for high and that you also might be beat for low. Nevertheless, betting is correct. If your opponent busts out on the end, or perhaps makes only a small pair, there is a good chance that he will fold, especially if the pot is not big. This bet may permit you to win the whole pot instead of getting only half of it.

As you can see, there are advantages to disguising your hand. If your opponent thinks you have a low when you actually have a high, expect to get paid off. And sometimes when you are going low, if you make your opponent think you are going high, you can bluff him out if you miss your low. Keep in mind that this type of bluffing play is risky and is usually successful only in the tighter games against tighter, but not necessarily better, players. However, some of the better players will fold too often in these spots, as they do not see this type of play very often.

The Later Streets

Afterthought

As you have seen, seven-card stud eight-or-better is a game of implied odds. It usually doesn't just cost one or two more bets to go to the river. From fifth street on, it can cost as much as seven to ten bets. This is a function of the cards that are out and the players that you are against. The implied odds are especially related to whether you can win all or only half of the pot.

Keep in mind that some of the biggest mistakes are made on fourth street. If your hand develops poorly, you should get out quickly. Staying to see another card can prove costly.

There are a few other things worth mentioning. To begin with, as the text points out, check-raising is very important in this game. Its main purpose is not always just to gain an extra bet, but also to be able to knock out an opponent and sometimes to win a pot that you otherwise wouldn't win. This is the real value of check-raising.

Disguising your hand can be crucial. You may not have many opportunities to do this, but when you can, it is a big money-maker. Always be thinking about how you might play your hand, so you can take maximum advantage when you are able to disguise it.

As for the high hands, keep in mind that if they look as though they can win only half the pot, many of them should be discarded on fifth street. Don't fall into the trap of automatically going all the way with a big pair.

And finally, don't be afraid to bet on seventh street in situations where a lot of your opponents will check. It's true that the potential action can be scary, but the bets that I have discussed are profitable.

Part Three

Miscellaneous Topics

Miscellaneous Topics

Introduction

So far, a lot of different subjects have been discussed in this section of *High-Low-Split Poker*. Yet in seven-card stud eight-or-better, many unique situations and possibilities can occur. Consequently, it is now time to address some miscellaneous topics, plus to clarify many of the concepts that already have been covered.

Some of these ideas have never been correctly discussed in print. This is also true of much of the information that follows. In fact, since so little has been written on stud high-low split eight-or-better, a great deal of this material will be new to a lot of readers.

Many of these concepts are not easy to comprehend, but once you master them, you can consider yourself an expert player — provided, that is, that you acquire the experience that is so necessary in achieving success in this game. As noted previously, there is no substitute for experience, and improving your judgment through learning is critical. A small error in judgment can trap you for a lot of bets or perhaps allow someone else to escape who could have been trapped for those bets instead.

Keep in mind that many of the following concepts interact with some of the other concepts and ideas already covered. One of the keys to successful seven-card stud eight-or-better is the ability to correctly assess the situation you are in. For example, being able to gauge that you are against two high hands and a low hand, as opposed to two low hands and a high hand, may dramatically alter your strategy. Developing the skills that enable you to make this type of assessment does not come easy. In time, however, such expertise can be achieved.

Position

Position is very important in seven-card stud eight-or-better, and being last to act is most advantageous. Since a lot of pots are raised, reraised, and jammed, acting last gives you an opportunity to know how expensive it will be to see the next card. It helps greatly for the high hand to be on your left. This increases your chances of being in last position, where you are most likely to also have an opportunity to make a skillful play, such as knocking the high hand out with a double bet.

This positional strength thus gives you two advantages. First, you may be able to bluff or squeeze out an opponent. Second — and more important — you can avoid those spots where you put in a bet or two and then later discover that there have been too many additional raises for you to call again. In other games, rarely must you put in one or two bets in a round and still have to fold. But in seven-card stud eight-or-better, this happens often when you are in an early position. With these additional bets behind you, it becomes obvious that either you are drawing dead or you are in very bad shape. You will have to fold, and you'll wish you had never made the previous call.

In most other games, if you put in two bets, you usually have enough outs to keep playing. But in this game, the fact that certain players are raising or reraising means that they have a cinch and you cannot win.

In conclusion, if your position is poor — especially if there are aggressive players behind you — you should give up on many of your marginal hands. However, if you are last to act and it is only one bet to you, many of these holdings can be played.

Playing the High Hands

The best high hand is a good starting hand, but holding the second-best high hand is one of the worst situations to be in. This is especially true if there are also low hands out against you. Thus, when you play a high hand, you have to be very sure that it is the best high hand out.

If you are the high hand and are playing heads up against a low hand, you sometimes will have to make a tough decision about folding on fifth street. This usually occurs when the player who started low catches two more low cards. In this case, you frequently will be folding the high hand, unless you have improved to at least two pair. If you do improve, you usually have to go to the river and just pay it off, even though you will lose many of these hands. However, a lot of times you will win, because the player going for low will have made two pair, or a pair and a low draw, but will not have completed the low. When this happens, you will scoop the pot.

Even though you will be playing the hand blindly — that is, you won't know where you stand — it essentially becomes a showdown. You can't make the mistake of folding just because your opponent has a scary board.

You should play high hands very strongly when there are other high cards out, as you are trying to trap the second- and third-best high hands and are hoping to drive out the low hands.

Most of the time when you are playing a high hand heads up against a probable low hand on third street, you have either raised or called a raise (or a reraise). If the low hand now catches an ace on fourth street and his other low card is a wheel card, it usually is correct to fold immediately. But you sometimes can make a "crying call" and then must be prepared to fold on fifth street if your opponent catches anything that looks as though it could be trouble or if your hand falls slightly dead.

This is one of the tough situations that comes up in this game, and there is no substitute for experience in helping you to determine the right course of action. You almost certainly are facing either a pair of aces or four low cards. Consequently, when you are against a player who you believe started with three low cards and he immediately catches an ace, it is usually best to fold your big pairs.

Also, if an opponent who appears to be going low pairs his door card on fourth street and bets, you should fold. This is especially true if a likely hand for this player is a small pair with an ace kicker. Now you could be facing trips. But even if you are not against three of a kind, your opponent will have playing advantages over you, and since the pot is still fairly small, it is usually best to get out.

When the second-best high hand is in the pot and you have the best high hand, you want to punish him. However, once a lot of money is put in early, you must be prepared to go to the river.

When there could be two low hands out against you, try to avoid putting in a lot of money early with a high hand. On a later street, you can get caught in a raising war and get punished, because the large pot makes it difficult to get away from your hand.

The time to push a high hand is when you are against another high hand (but not one as good as yours) and a low draw. This is one of the better situations, though it may not always seem so. Obviously, it is also a good situation for the low hand. But it is not as good as most everyone thinks, because the low hand frequently will bust out and you'll scoop the pot.

Bluffing

In stud eight-or-better, bluffing takes a slightly different form. Generally you are not bluffing to win the whole pot, except perhaps with an ante steal or a bluff on fourth street, where your lone opponent has busted out and you merely steal the pot.

When you are bluffing, usually by raising or check-raising, you typically are attempting to knock out another hand that you don't want to contest your way. This may be a slightly better hand or a hand that you think is about equal to yours. That is, you are not bluffing to win the pot; you are bluffing to win your half of the pot.

There are exceptions, but they are rare. When playing heads up, if you miss on the end, think your lone opponent might also have missed on the end, and don't think he will call with a small pair, then you may bluff trying to win the whole pot. But this type of play does not occur very often.

Sometimes a good bluffing opportunity comes up on the end when it looks as though you were drawing at a high hand, such as a flush, or it is obvious that you had two pair or trips and were jammed in on sixth street by what appears to be a straight and a lock low. On the river, the low bets and you raise, the player with the straight calls, the low reraises, and you raise again. On rare occasions, you will convince the player who holds the better high hand that he is beat, and he will throw his cards away.

This is one of the few times that a bluff will work. But notice that you are bluffing for only half the pot, and you must commit a lot of chips. In addition, you have to be very cautious of whom you use this play against. Most players will call the double bet, because the pot has become so big that they feel compelled to call. But there are some players who will muck their hands.

After you've successfully made this play, you must realize that since your hand gets shown, your opponents will see what you have done. Thus, you won't be able to make this bluff again — at least against these same players — for quite a while.

Slow-Playing

One of the few times that you might want to slow-play is when you have a low hand that is not likely to be beat. Since you can win only half the pot, this becomes a good time to draw other players in.

For example, suppose you have a

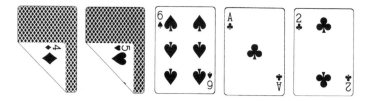

made on fifth street. You are in a multiway pot, there are no other completed lows, two or three treys are dead, and no one has what could be a wheel draw. Since someone most likely will have to catch perfect twice to beat your hand, you may want to slow-play and get some extra customers.

The exception to slow-playing is if you think a bet or raise may drive out everyone except another low hand. Now you might be able to make a small pair — or just catch a high card — and scoop the pot. Also, notice that if you get beat for low in this spot, since your opponent must catch low cards, your chances of winning high with a weak hand go up (as long as your opponent does not make a wheel).

However, if you have a high draw to go along with your low hand, you may want to play hard and fast, since you also have a chance to win high. For instance, in the example just given, if the treys were all live, you probably would not want to slow-play your hand.

When holding a high hand, you should not slow-play, as you have a chance to win the whole pot if no one makes the low.

Consequently, you don't want to encourage too many low hands to come in against you.

When you have a very big high hand, such as a full house or an ace-high flush, that is not likely to be beat by what you see out against you, it becomes correct to slow-play when it's obvious that a low has been made and you know this player will stay to the end. Since you are going to split anyway, you may want to slow down, as it doesn't pay to drive out players at this point.

But if there is any chance that a low has not yet been made, it is best to eliminate players. This is especially true if someone else has a chance to make a high hand and beat you. Now you hope to get to play against a busted low hand, which is one of your bigger earns.

Knowing Your Opponents

In seven-card stud eight-or-better, you will have an advantage that you don't always have in other games. By knowing how different players play — and advanced players usually have a good idea as to how well their opponents play and what their styles are — you generally can qualify your opponent's hand.

For instance, when a tight player comes in with a raise, it usually means he has either a high hand and is trying to limit the field or a very strong low hand and is trying to get more money into the pot. So this is a time when you should be cautious and avoid coming in with the second-best hand. You should throw away hands that look fairly good under ordinary circumstances, because now they are not even marginal.

The exception to discarding your hand is if you know a player extremely well. For example, if you are virtually certain that your opponent has a high hand, even if a low card is up — that is, he raises only with big pairs in the hole — you can call with a questionable low hand. By the same token, if you know he raises only with low hands and you have a high hand, you can reraise, limit the field, play heads up against him, and have an edge.

Here's another example. Suppose you are against a player who automatically plays high three flushes and high three straights. Either his hand will turn into a bust, whereupon you get to jam him with a low hand, or you will get jammed. When you oppose this type of player, you want to have a very good hand that can survive the jamming, because jamming often will develop. Also, when your high hands improve to two pair, they can get jammed in if your opponent catches his straight or flush card. You don't always know where you stand, because he might be betting with a high pair.

In the end, a player who plays this loose is going to lose. But if you don't play properly and adjust your play when one of these players is in, you also will lose.

In addition, you are going to play against a lot of different kinds of players in this game. When you play hold 'em, you usually are just playing against hold 'em players, and when you play stud, you are usually against those people who play only seven-card stud. But when playing seven-card stud eight-or-better, you often will find yourself competing against a lot of players whose strongest game is either seven-card stud or razz, against some people who play many games, and against a few who specialize in this game. This leads to some interesting strategy adjustments.

Specifically, seven-card stud players tend to play high hands strongly and to stay with them longer than do razz players or more experienced eight-or-better players. Consequently, when you are against a seven-card stud player, keep in mind that he usually will be aggressive with big pairs but cautious with weaker low hands.

A razz player will do just the opposite. He frequently will be extremely aggressive with low hands, especially if they have straight possibilities. In fact, it is not unusual to see a razz player play these types of hands absolutely to the limit. But with high hands, he will be less aggressive when facing hands with low possibilities.

The top eight-or-better players have a good mix to their games. This makes it much tougher to know exactly where they stand. They will play low hands both fast and slow. They will do the same with high hands, assuming they play them — which they may not do a lot in certain games, unless their holdings are premium high hands.

But there are many players who tend to play more one way than the other. For example, when the table is full, some players will play very tight, plus the few hands that they do play are almost all high-quality low hands that are often three straights.

When one of these players catches perfect on fourth street, you should not give him any action. This is because he has either a pair or a straight draw, as well as the low draw. However, this type of player usually will tell you exactly what his hand is by how he now plays it. If he checks, he is paired; if he bets out into several players or raises, he has caught good.

Many stud eight-or-better players are very consistent in their play. For example, some people are always aggressive on third street with good low hands; others will wait until fifth street to see what they have made.

It is also usually easier to know where someone stands by his show of weakness rather than of strength. This is especially true of aggressive players, who are frequently difficult to read on an early street.

Raising Aggressively

Most of the time in seven-card stud eight-or-better, the reasons to play aggressively are both to get more money into the pot and to drive other players out. If you have a terrific hand like a wheel, then you may be betting or raising just to make the pot bigger. But in general, this will not be the case. You won't be bluffing very often, and you won't raise as a bluff. But you occasionally will raise to set up a play, to disguise your hand, or to knock someone out. Sometimes you can raise to get a free card, but this won't often be advantageous, as many of your opponents will raise back. Moreover, the free cards that you get won't have the potential, as they do in many other games, to make a big disguised hand.

Also, when you raise, you won't get a lot of information. When people have a playable hand, they usually hang on; if they don't, they generally fold. So raising won't define the strength of an opponent's hand very well.

The few times that raising does gain you information, it is often the type of information that you could do without. That is, you usually will find yourself calling a reraise. Now your raise had better have been on a very strong hand, since you have just put a lot of money in the pot and frequently will be forced to play to the end because of your action.

The Toughest Decision of All

Suppose you have what seems to be the best low hand and are forcing the action. Now on sixth or seventh street, it appears as though an opponent catches a card that could make you the second-best low hand or could even cause you to be drawing dead. However, you are not sure that this is the case. After having put in a lot of bets, you are faced with what is probably the toughest decision in this game — that is, whether to fold or not.

Normally, it is best to bet the hand and hope that your opponent is going the opposite direction from you or that the card in question paired him. If he raises (no matter what the high hand does) or reraises, and he is a player without much imagination, it's best to throw your hand away, unless you have a quality draw to beat him. If he is a player with a lot of imagination or flair, who might be making a move on you, then you may want to continue playing. You might raise back and see whether you get raised again. If you do, you almost always should fold, since very few players have the nerve to make a play such as this.

When in this situation, you must read the cards very well and, of course, know your opponent. If you are not accomplished in these areas, you might discover that the miracle card your opponent caught made him a high hand and that you have thrown away a lock for low. Accurately assessing this type of situation is one of those areas in which advanced players excel.

Staying to the End

Many players will get into trouble by automatically staying to the end when they have four good low cards, meaning a good draw at a low, regardless of what is out against them. Usually, you stay to the end when you are trying to make the best low or a hand that has a reasonable chance of being the best low but is also an inside straight draw or better. But there are times when you should throw these hands away, such as when your hand is not very live, the pot odds you are getting are not very good, or the chances are high that you'll make your hand but it will not be the best hand.

A lot of chips go into the pot in these games, and one advantage you will have is that the dealers often stack the chips as the hand proceeds. This allows you to keep track of how much money is in the pot and will give you an approximation of what each half of the pot will pay. In other words, you should have a good idea of what the current pot odds are, as well as what your implied pot odds will be.

Pairing the Door Card

If you are going high and pair your door card, you most likely have made trips. Now you should bet out and continue betting most of the way through the hand. If someone is raising, you probably should be reraising, unless it looks as though there is a good chance you are beat. Usually the raise will come from a low hand who has a player with a weaker low hand trapped in the middle. However, if the raise occurs in heads-up play and you are looking at three low cards, you could be beat or your opponent could have a free roll, so you should just call.

If you have a low card up, you pair your door card on fourth street, and it does not make you trips, it is actually an improvement, since you have slightly improved your winning chances. But it is not necessarily the improvement that you want. Pairing your door card is certainly better than receiving a bust card, in which case you probably would muck your hand, but it frequently does not add much value to your hand. It sometimes allows you to disguise your holding and perhaps to bluff a little, because your opponent may be scared of trips. Generally, the high card will take one more card off. If you then catch another low card, he usually will give up, unless he has made at least two pair. If you catch a bust on fifth street, the high hand almost always will play on, so you need trips or at least two pair to bet.

The bad part about pairing your door card when you have a low card up is that you probably will be first to act the rest of the way. If you are not first, it means that someone else has a bigger pair showing, in which case you are most likely beat and will have to go out.

If you are first and have a weak hand, your bet is virtually a bluff and you are hoping to knock out opponents. But pairing your small door card improves three low cards, because this enables you to catch any low card, a trip card, or another pair to likely give you the best hand in one of the directions.

If you are up against other low hands, pairing your small door card puts you at a definite disadvantage. If you are up against a high hand, it doesn't matter, because you will be trying to mislead him anyway.

If you pair your low door card and make trips, you generally should play your hand as you would if you had made big trips. That is, bet it all the way — unless someone makes a scary board, in which case you will either check and call, check and raise (if you make a full house or better), or check and fold (if it is obvious your opponent has made a better hand, such as higher trips). If you have a big pair in the hole, you usually should bet it all the way through and hope that someone does not beat you.

When your opponent pairs his small door card, he typically has three low cards with a pair or two big pair, especially if he is a tight player, in which case you have to play accordingly. It is less likely that he has trips than the other two hands.

However, if your opponent is a tight player and continues to play very aggressively, he usually does have three of a kind or the two big pair. If he has a pair and three low cards, he might bet his hand on fourth street to see what happens. But if he catches a bust card on fifth street, he will likely check and fold.

If he catches another low card on fifth street and bets, you are against trips, two big pair, or four low cards with a pair. In any case, his hand is fairly strong. If you have only a high pair or four low cards, he is the favorite over you and you easily can be scooped.

As you can see, when your opponent pairs his door card, it is not as dangerous in this game as it is in high-only seven-card stud. But it is still not a card that you want him to catch, as you are now at a disadvantage and it will require some thought as to how you want to play.

However, if the player on your immediate right in a multiway pot pairs his door card, it puts you at a significant disadvantage during the hand. This is especially true if he is an aggressive player, or if he is a weak player who is liable to keep betting without the best hand just because he is high. You may have a lot of problems in the play of the hand, since you might find yourself jammed in on a later round. Thus to play on, you must have helped your hand considerably on both fourth street and fifth street.

In addition, the player who paired his door card may have made trips, which usually will make him a big favorite to win high. Even if you have a low hand, you will lose a lot of your equity. This is because if you also make a straight or a flush, it is not as likely that you'll win both ways.

Finally, when you pair your door card on fourth street, you do not have the option of making either a single or a double-sized bet. You can make only the single bet, or you can check. Notice that this reduces your advantage, since you don't have the option to make the big bet that might drive some players out.

Keeping Track of the Cards

It's vitally necessary that you keep track of the cards, especially the low cards. Many situations will develop where you need one or two cards to make your hand and outdraw a better low hand, or you will need to know how live certain cards are to determine whether it is likely that an opponent will have a particular hand that you might be scared of.

For example, suppose you have a six-high straight and are worried about whether an opponent might have a split with you or a possible wheel. Knowing where the cards lie and remembering them will have a large effect on whether you jam or not. You sometimes will see this with players who can't remember all the cards. For instance, they may not recall that a fourth deuce was folded earlier, which could mean that the hand they are calling with is a lock and they should be raising instead.

You also can deduce a great deal about the cards you don't see. Suppose, for example, that someone starts with a low card up, meaning that he probably is going low. If he folds after catching another low card, such as a deuce — which could have given him four good cards — you can conclude that two deuces are gone. This information might help you later, especially in determining whether you have a lock. Consequently, paying close attention to what is folded can be crucial. Knowing that one or two key cards are dead sometimes can make the difference between a raising hand and one that you will just play along with.

Scare Cards

If you play a lot of seven-card stud straight high, you will realize that scare cards are indeed scary. But they don't always help the hand. Most of the time, all that a scare card does is provide you with more opportunities for improvement. So a scare card adds value to your hand, even though there is a good chance that it does not actually help your hand.

However, in stud eight-or better, scare cards usually do improve your hand. This is because hands in eight-or-better are less disguised and are almost always built around the upcard. Consequently, a scare card is a card that you are playing for.

(In high-only stud, your hand is less likely to be built around your upcard. Put another way, your upcard in eight-or-better is more of a key card than it is in straight seven-card stud.)

An Expert Play

Suppose you start with four low cards and are playing heads up against a mediocre high hand, such as a high pair. You believe your opponent has put you on this hand, and on fifth street, you catch a high card. You can now check-raise. Any player in his right mind will not think you are going to check-raise with just four low cards, so he will now assume that you have a high hand.

If he thinks you have made trips, or perhaps just two big pair, he might throw his hand away. Should this happen, you have made a great play. If he calls and you make an open pair on sixth street, you can bet out again. There is a good chance that he will fold in this spot, fearing that he may be drawing dead. If you catch another low card, he probably will continue to play, although he may go out if he fears a straight.

A continuation of this complicated play is that if you catch a garbage card on sixth street, you should check. Your opponent will now put you on a four-card straight and will figure that you've missed. Since he won't want to give you a free card, he will bet and you can check-raise him again. Now your opponent should be fairly convinced that he has run into a good high hand. Even if he calls, he probably won't pay it off on the river.

Keep in mind that the check-raise on sixth street will work only against a player who will bet his hand. If you are against someone who is timid and who is likely to check on sixth street, this play probably will fail. So don't try it.

One reason that check-raising on fifth and sixth streets gives you the best of it is because your hand is camouflaged and your opponent's hand is not. (This is a disadvantage of playing heads up with a high hand that hasn't improved.) However, if your opponent's board becomes scary, you must be careful about putting too much money in the pot.

83

Another Good Play

In a three-way pot on fifth street, suppose one player has an obvious high hand, you have four low cards and make a small open pair, and the third player appears to have made his low. If you check, the high hand probably will check, the low hand will bet, and you can now raise.

Since it is obvious that you don't have a low hand, and since you are raising into the high hand, he will put you on at least two pair and probably trips. (In stud eight-or-better, when someone makes a small open pair, most opponents will be scared of trips since starting with three low cards is common.) Your raise usually will knock out the high hand, enabling you to play heads up against the low hand. In addition, the low hand often will be afraid that you may back into a low and beat him. Thus he is not likely to raise back. If he does go to three bets, there is a good chance that he has an additional draw with his low. Notice that if you make your low hand, you may scoop the pot if your small pair holds up for high.

Many good players use this play. But even if you suspect it, when someone raises or check-raises into you with an open pair, you can't continue playing with a high pair, since the low is already made. You are being forced to lay 2-to-1 odds, and you are playing for only half the pot.

Quick Notes

Many people often become exasperated when playing stud eight-or-better. They will have four low cards and keep catching bad cards. Or they will have a high hand, the low hands will catch dangerous cards, and the situation will get scary. By watching players' reactions, you can get a good read on their hands. You will see which way they are looking and who they are worried about.

You can get similar information from how they play their hands. For instance, if one of the low hands improves to a probable second-best low on a later street, you often will see this player make a frustrated call, which will provide a good indication as to how strong he is.

Stud eight-or-better is not a good game for steamers, since they definitely will go too far with their hands and will put too much money in the pot. But they won't do much raising, except perhaps on third street. This means that if you see someone who is on tilt start jamming on a later street, he has a good hand, as it is just too easy to be locked up.

♣ ♦ ♥ ♠

In seven-card stud eight-or-better, it is more difficult to psych people out than it is in a one-winner type of game. This is because your opponent often believes he can always win the other half of the pot. Thus, being extremely aggressive and showing strength don't help you as much as they would in a one-winner game, since players won't get as scared and fold as often.

From an image point of view, rather than have people fear you (except perhaps on the first three cards), you would prefer them to tag along, so you can scoop them on big pots and maybe get them to make some bad plays near the end. Notice that this is the opposite type of image from what you want to have in most standard games. Remember, your image must fit your style of play, or you may be the one who is off-balance. Moreover, the image you project may need to be changed according to the conditions of the game.

♣ ♦ ♥ ♠

Sometimes near the end of a hand, players will start jamming, and it will look fairly certain that better high and low hands are out against you. That is, you may now find yourself caught in the middle, even though you had the best hand all the way through. Unless you think you are against a player who not only will bluff but is likely to be doing so now, you are most certainly beat.

If the jamming starts on sixth street, this may be a time when it will cost you at least four or five bets on the end, and perhaps even as many as ten bets. In this spot, you can't be stubborn, and you may have to throw away a very strong hand. Remember, it can be expensive for you to see the end of the hand when your hand is probably second-best.

♣ ♦ ♥ ♠

Live cards can never be overemphasized, especially when you have the high hand. A common situation on fifth street is to be high with a big pair and be up against a four-card low hand with a pair. Your high hand now must be live, because you often will run into two pair on the end and you must be able to beat this hand.

When high, you have to start with very live cards and you must be prepared to fold if your cards start falling dead. In multiway pots, small two-pair hands will come up frequently, and you will need a live hand to withstand the heat if the action picks up. (See *Seven-Card Stud For Advanced Players* for more discussion on this topic.)

♣ ♦ ♥ ♠

In seven-card stud eight-or-better, unlike in many other forms of poker, inducing bluffs is almost impossible. But you sometimes can get a player to bet a slightly weaker hand, which you can then check-raise. The typical player usually is happy to check down his hand when he doesn't have much and is very happy to get a free card when he is weak.

♣ ♦ ♥ ♠

Reading hands is very important in this game, as it is in all poker games. In Texas hold 'em, for instance, the flop can change the value of your hand significantly, and in seven-card stud, hands are changed by the scare cards. But in stud eight-or-better, hands don't change very much. Players appearing to go low usually make low hands, and players appearing to go high usually make high hands. As an example, if someone starts with a king up, he probably will show you a high hand if he plays to the end.

This means that getting a read on a player early in the hand is crucial, even though some of the apparent low hands change or can conceal high hands. But the way a person plays his hand early on should give away his foundation, and the advanced player can use this information later. So it is important to put someone on a hand early, and then to well-define this hand on a later street when the big money goes in.

♣ ♦ ♥ ♠

When you start with three good low cards and catch bad on fourth street, it is generally correct to fold, as long as the pot is not too big. Some players automatically will fold in this situation. When you are against these players, you always should raise on third street, even if you think you have slightly the worst hand. If they catch bad on fourth street and fold as expected, you have gained equity.

On the other hand, some players who start with three small cards will always call on fourth street, even when they catch bad. Now to gain equity, you want to keep the pot as small as possible. You gain by folding correctly on fourth street when they don't.

Miscellaneous Topics
Afterthought

Even though seven-card stud eight-or-better is not considered to be as complex as some of the other forms of poker, there is still a lot to this game. Just consider all the topics that have been covered in this section alone. In fact, this book never can be totally complete, because there are so many possible situations that you can find yourself in, and everyone plays differently from everyone else.

Keep in mind that stud eight-or-better is a game of tough decisions. The pots sometimes get very big, and it can be extremely difficult to throw your hand away. Nevertheless, you must make some of these folds, because either you are beat or the price you have to pay to finish the hand is too high.

It's also necessary to disguise your hand whenever possible. This has been stressed at other points in the text but bears mentioning again. To win those occasional big pots that you normally would not win, you must throw off your opponents. This is true when playing against the better players, and it is true against weaker players. However, remember that it is much tougher to trick the experts, since they understand many of the plays.

Finally, a lot of the strategies that have been discussed are correct only when the situation and conditions are right. Don't fall into the trap of making great plays just to make great plays. You should be trying to win the most money, not to impress everyone at the table.

Part Four

The Game Itself

The Game Itself

Introduction

Since seven-card stud eight-or-better doesn't get spread in major cardrooms as often as some of the other forms of poker, the game can vary a great deal. Sometimes you will be sitting with mostly experts; at other times, several weak players may be present. And — as we will see is also true in Omaha eight-or-better — the high-limit games play differently from the smaller games (though not, in general, to the same degree).

In addition, the character of the game that you are in can change very quickly. This is especially true during the major tournaments, where many seven-card stud eight-or-better games still appear, since players in the side games frequently play only for a short period of time.

In any case, to be successful, you must be able to make the appropriate strategy changes that are required. Although many of the concepts already discussed will still apply, some changes need to be pointed out.

Playing in Tight Games

Very often during a game, your opponents will change. That is, players will come and go. Sometimes the game you are in will become very tight. When this happens, you generally should leave (and perhaps use the time to reread this book). But if the game is tight and non-aggressive, then you are in a good situation. You can steal some antes, and you will be able to get in cheap and do some bluffing on fourth and fifth streets when you catch scare cards.

Of course, when one of your tight opponents comes in, he will have a quality starting hand. If he catches a scare card, you usually should go out, unless your hand has substantially improved. This is most important when you are in the pot with a weaker hand.

In these tight games, most of the hands that you will be playing past the opening bet are the best high hands and good low hands. These are the hands that have a lot of value in this type of game. However, be careful about going too far, because when you get challenged, you frequently will be up against a premium hand. Remember, you will make most of your money by stealing antes or by stealing on fourth street, since a lot of players will fold after taking one card off.

However, you generally want to avoid extremely tight but aggressive games. In eight-or-better, many of your opponents will be competent players, especially if they are playing fairly tight. So you won't have much of an edge against them, if you have an edge at all.

This brings us to an interesting conclusion: It may be all right to play in one of these games, providing that you do not play for very long. You might steal a few antes and perhaps make a couple of plays. But competent players — who may be caught off-guard at first — will soon catch on, and your advantage will diminish, if not disappear altogether. The exception to playing for only a short time is if some weak players are waiting to get into the game. In this case, you might want to stay.

It should be clear that high hands go up in value in tight games, since most of the pots are heads up and the hands don't always go to the river. However, most players fold high hands too quickly (usually around fifth street) when they see a low hand developing, because they don't want to put in a lot of money and only split the pot. They forget that there often is already a significant amount of money in the pot, and since the action is usually heads up, they have the option of just checking and calling.

By the same token, it is easy to go too far with a high hand in a tight game, where you might be against a better high hand. Now you will be playing high against high with the worst hand. This is especially true if your opponent has an ace up or if he catches an ace.

Playing in Loose Games

When you are playing at a smaller limit, the game sometimes will be looser than what you generally see. If you are lucky enough to be in this situation, seven-card stud eight-or-better becomes a great game.

Since there are only a relatively small number of good multiway starting hands, this means that a lot of your opponents will be playing small pairs, second-best high hands, and weak non-connected low cards. In this case, all the good hands go up in value, and you should make a lot of money by just playing quality starting hands in a straightforward manner.

Hands that have two-way possibilities, such as small flush cards and small straight cards, go up in value. But high hands usually drop in value, because more lows will be made (since there are more people in the pots), plus it will be very hard to rate your hand and know how to play it correctly.

When you are playing in games like this, you should tighten up rather than loosen up. In many other forms of poker, you can play some slightly weaker hands when the games are loose, but doing this in seven-card stud eight-or-better is a major error. You won't be able to ante-steal, so you should discard just about all of your small pairs, and you also should throw away most of your medium and high pairs. This limits you to the very strongest high hands, to low hands that are connected for straights and flushes, and to low hands that have an ace. When playing in this manner, your average starting hand will tend to be much bigger than normal. This means that you will be betting and raising just to get more money into the pot.

Also, your opponents will be turning up unexpected cards, which will make many players hard to read. Although you should be able to at least determine whether they are going high or low, it will be much more difficult to put them on specific hands. Consequently, you should tend to play straightforward, and when you think you have the best hand, get your money in the pot. Either bet or raise, but don't attempt any tricky plays.

However, when your hand is weak, try to play for as little as possible. And if you bust out on fourth street, be willing to see fifth street more often than you normally would, since the pot odds for staying in frequently will be larger. In addition, you should make bigger hands and have more potential for multiway scoops.

Playing Short-Handed

For some reason, more players walk in stud eight-or-better than in almost any other form of poker, and your table frequently will not be full unless the game is very good. Consequently, you must be skilled at playing short-handed, much more so in this game than in other games.

When playing short-handed, high hands go up in value and the game becomes more like seven-card stud, with the high hands contesting each other. Low hands that have high possibilities also go up in value, and high hands with low possibilities, even though they may not be the greatest lows, go up in value even more.

The hands that you want to stay away from are low hands that have no straight or flush possibilities, unless you are playing as a complete bluff. But if the game is fairly tight and short-handed, which is typical of many games, most of your opponents will throw away their hands on fourth street if you catch good and they don't. This will give you some bluffing opportunities.

Big Games
Versus Small Games

Keep in mind that in seven-card stud eight-or-better, as the limits get higher, the players usually get better. Although this is true in all poker games, it is especially true in this game.

In the big games, when players start jamming on the later streets, they are almost always correct to do so. This is not the case at the smaller limits. In these games, someone occasionally may be jamming with the worst hand, perhaps because a concealed better hand is out.

But in the bigger games, players read the cards very well, and when they do jam, they are most often right. Thus at the higher limits, the person doing the jamming generally wins the pot, unless someone gets lucky with a draw.

Of course, a very creative player may do some jamming to knock an opponent out of the pot, but this is a different situation. Even when you recognize that you are in this spot, it still may be correct to fold, as it will be extremely expensive to see the hand all the way through, plus you can't be too sure of the situation.

In the smaller games, more players are typically in each hand, meaning that the pots may be proportionately larger for the betting limit than in the big games. But in the big games, it usually costs more per individual (in terms of units bet) to see a hand all the way through, as the players are better able to capitalize on those spots where it is correct to raise and reraise or to jam.

Many times in the smaller games, a player who has the high and another player who has the low don't jam, because they don't perceive exactly where they stand. Thus, there may be only a bet and a call on each round, where it should have been jammed all the way through. In the high-stakes games (around $50-$100 and above), don't expect the better players to make this kind of mistake. They will seize these opportunities and force you to pay the maximum when you are in the pot without the best hand.

Running the Game

In seven-card stud eight-or-better, because of the large split pots and the difficulty in accurately reading hands, it is common for there to be several dealer errors during a playing session. Consequently, if you are not paying close attention, you may get the worst of it.

In many cases, it's necessary for the players to assist the dealer in running the game and to make sure that he or she does the job properly. But this doesn't mean that dealers should be screamed at when they make mistakes. Such behavior only serves to make some dealers upset and nervous, and the game will be ruined as a result.

When required, you should politely explain the proper procedures to those dealers who may be unfamiliar with stud eight-or-better. It may even be necessary to delegate one player as the "table captain," so to speak, who will take on the responsibility of ensuring that the game is run properly.

Dealers should never be allowed to "play with the pot." When splitting a pot, the dealer should split the bills first, then the biggest chips, and then the rest of the chips in descending order down to the smallest denomination. This is very important, as when the pot is divided in a haphazard manner, it's tough to determine whether the split is correct.

The players also may need to instruct a dealer that when three or more people are in the pot and the action has stopped, the dealer should rake all the bets into the center. He or she then should divide the pot when either the hand is over or there is a slowdown in the action.

If a pot becomes heads up, the procedure is different. Now any additional bets should remain near the players' hands, and the dealer should not touch the chips except to verify the amounts. If the pot is split, the players take their bets back, and the dealer needs to divide only what already was in the middle. If there is only one winner, the dealer will push that person the whole pot. By adhering to these procedures, the bets are always kept straight.

Normally, only the dealer should split the pot. But there is an exception. When two players agree to split, which they sometimes do in smaller pots, one of them usually will say something like, "Push it to me and we will chop it up." If the house allows this, the dealer should push the pot to one of the players and let that player do the splitting.

This practice should be permitted as long as the pot is being contested heads up. If it is not allowed, the players may just check the hands down and then split the pot later. But the dealer should not do the splitting when two players mutually agree to "chop it." The dealer should push the pot to one of the players, and the players should then split the pot between themselves. Notice that the house has no further responsibility for the split.

In addition, any player at the table has the right to see the hands when the pot is "chopped." If this request is made, the players should turn their hands face up for viewing, and the dealer should then get on with the game.

Players should be in the habit of stacking their bets so they can be seen as individual bets. This is much better than putting all the bets in a pile, which will require the dealer to break them down.

Another habit that all players should acquire is to announce their entire hands on the end when there is a bet and a call. For example, you should say something like, "Eights up for high and an eight for low."

Failing to announce your entire hand not only will slow down the game, but also can be very irritating. For instance, it is not uncommon for the bettor to announce, "I have a seven for low," then the caller to say, "I have two pair for high," and then the bettor to state, "I also have trips for high."

I recognize that it is not the dealer's job to tell players that they should call their complete hands. But there is no reason why some players cannot politely encourage other players to do this. By the way, you are not expected to be the only player at the table who is polite. If no one else will call his complete hand, then you might as well call only one side of your hand.

Also, when the hand is over, make sure that you call your hand rather than just turn it face up. Otherwise the dealer will have to sift through your cards to determine what you've made. This encourages dealer errors, plus the dealer has to take his attention away from the pot and the other players' hands. In gambling, anything can happen. By not calling your hand, you are increasing the chances that things can go wrong — not so much by cheating, but by mistakes that can be made.

In addition, it is helpful to arrange your cards so they are visually easy to read. This way, the dealer won't have to touch your hand. If you do nothing but turn your cards face up, it is always possible that the dealer will overlook your hand, pick it up, and then muck it. If this happens, you have no one to blame but yourself when your opponent stacks all the chips.

Seven-card stud eight-or-better, like high-only stud, is an ante game. That is, the antes should be in front of every player and then raked into the center of the table before the dealer deals. The first card should not come off the deck until all the antes are in the pot and together.

A dealer should never deal the hand and then say to someone, "You're light." The custom is for the dealer to request players to ante, and if a player fails to act, he should be dealt out. There is no reason for the dealer to ask two or three times for a player to ante unless it is likely that the player did not hear the dealer's request.

In stud eight-or-better, some players who lose two or three hands in a row like to sit out a hand. Usually they are trying to change their luck or to change the run of the cards, which by the way is complete nonsense. However, when a dealer keeps asking one of these players to ante, it not only will irritate that player, but will slow down the game as well. The dealer should ask once, and then deal if the player doesn't respond.

A dealer should never reach into your stack and take off an ante to put you in. In fact, a dealer should not touch your chips at any time, nor should a player ever touch another player's chips.

However, this is often done in the bigger games, because most high-limit players trust each other. Through the years, there has not been much of a problem with this practice.

The Game Itself

Afterthought

As you can see, many of the ideas presented in this section are built upon those concepts covered earlier in the book. For example, playing in short-handed games is similar to, though not the same as, playing in a full game after several people have passed.

When you sit down to seven-card stud eight-or-better, you should ask yourself, "How aggressive is this game?" As has been pointed out, if the game is tight and aggressive, you probably should leave. But a tight and passive game is reasonably profitable once you have become an expert player.

Also, you will recall that there was a great deal of discussion in this section concerning how a seven-card stud eight-or-better game should be run. Don't underestimate the value of this information. Much of your "earn" will come from having the opportunity to play a lot of hands — that is, if the dealer is proficient in his or her job. You can help ensure that the game is conducted in an efficient manner, and it is frequently important that you do so. Otherwise the game often will slow down, errors might get made that could cause arguments, and some of your opponents may get out of a gambling mood. Put another way, you need to make sure that your bottom-line expectation will not be reduced.

Part Five
Other Skills

Other Skills

Introduction

There are two additional areas that play a major role in winning at seven-card stud eight-or-better (as well as at all forms of poker). They are reading hands and psychology.

Reading hands is both an art and a science. The same is true for correct applications of psychology at the poker table. In both instances, you must know your opponents. More specifically, the better you understand how your opponents think and thus how they play, the better you will be able to choose the correct strategies to use against them.

When you are not in a pot, it is still very important to pay attention to what is going on. By doing so, you will begin to understand how different opponents play their hands in different situations and what tactics they are most likely to try. Also, you can get a feel for how they think. You will see what they handle easily and what confuses them, and you will get an idea of what strategies work best against them.

Keep in mind that the concepts discussed in this section cannot be mastered quickly. Like many other skills at the seven-card stud eight-or-better table, reading hands and applying psychology take a while to learn. But once mastered, they will become a significant factor in your winning play. And for those of you who make it to the very big games (against the world champions), you must become an expert in these two areas to have any chance of success.

Reading Hands

Excellent techniques are available for reading hands in seven-card stud high-low-split eight-or-better. Most commonly, you analyze the meaning of an opponent's check, bet, or raise, and you look at the exposed cards and try to judge from them what his entire hand might be. You then combine the plays he has made *throughout the hand* with the exposed cards and come to a determination about his most likely hand.

In other words, you use logic to read hands. You interpret your opponents' plays on each round and note the cards that appear on the board, paying close attention to the order in which they appear. You then put these two pieces of evidence together — the plays and the cards on the board — to draw a conclusion about an opponent's most likely hand.

Sometimes you can put an opponent on a specific hand quite early. However, in general, it's a mistake to do this and then stick to your initial conclusion no matter how things develop. A player who raises on third street and then raises again after catching only small cards may have a big pair in the hole, but he also may be on a draw and is trying for a free card. Drawing a narrow, irreversible conclusion early can lead to costly mistakes later, such as giving that free card or betting into your opponent when he makes his hand.

What you should do is to put an opponent on a variety of hands at the start of play, and as play progresses, eliminate some of those hands based on his later play and on the cards he catches. Through this process of elimination, you should have a good idea of what that opponent has (or is drawing to) when the last card is dealt.

For instance, suppose on third street that you raise with a high card up and an opponent showing a small card calls your raise. On fourth street, he catches another small card close in rank to his upcard and bets after you check. You call, and on fifth street

107

you both catch blanks. When you check to him, he also checks. It is now likely that this player has only a three-card low with a small pair. If your opponent catches another low card on sixth street that appears to possibly give him a small straight, you should not fold. If he catches a blank on sixth street, you should bet and then probably bet again on the river if you make two pair, assuming that he did not fold on sixth street. In addition, if he catches good on sixth street, you should check and call on the river, since you still have a good shot at the high half of the pot. (In fact, if he misses again and fails to make a low, you might scoop the whole pot.)

However, if it turns out that you cannot beat a small pair (perhaps you started with a high three flush), you may now want to bet, since there is some chance that you can pick up the pot. This might happen if your opponent has missed his low and doesn't call you with one pair.

At the end of a hand, it becomes especially crucial to have a good idea of what your opponent has. The more accurately you can read hands, the better you can determine what your chances are of having your opponent beat. This, of course, helps you in deciding how to play your hand.

In practice, most players at least try to determine whether an opponent has a bad hand, a mediocre hand, a good hand, or a great hand. For instance, let's say your opponent bets on the end. Usually when a person bets, it represents either a bluff, a good hand, or a great hand, but not a mediocre hand. If your opponent had a mediocre hand, he probably would check. If you have only a mediocre hand, you must determine what the chances are that your opponent is bluffing and whether those chances warrant a call in relation to the pot odds. For example, most players will not bet a rough low on the end if someone else also appears to be going low. This is the mediocre type hand that they hope will win the pot in a showdown.

We have seen that in seven-card stud eight-or-better, one way to read hands is to start by considering a variety of possible hands an opponent might have and then to eliminate some of those possibilities as the hand develops. A complementary way to read hands is to work backward. For instance, if someone with a small card up cold calls a raise and a reraise by a king and a small card, then catches medium-sized cards higher than an eight on fourth and fifth streets, but is able to raise on sixth street, you think back on his play in earlier rounds. Since it does not seem possible that he would have gone this far with something like a small three straight, you now have to suspect that he is rolled up.

Here is another example. Suppose on sixth street that a player who called a raise on third street has

Someone with a king in the door and a small pair on board bets; another player who caught an ace on sixth street and who has two other small cards up, both lower than a six, raises; and now this person calls the raise. What is his hand?

First, notice it is unlikely that this player just has a draw to a six. Given the cards showing in his opponents' hands, he may have only a small chance of winning even half the pot, since he is likely to be against a player who has him locked out of the high and another player who may have him locked out of both the high and the low. This means that he also has at least a gut-shot straight draw, but more probably a flush draw as well. There is a good chance that he has two small clubs in the hole.

Now for a third example. On third street, suppose several people with small cards up limp in, and the pot is then raised by a strong player with the 6♦ up. On fourth street, the strong player catches another small diamond, but one of the original limpers in an early position catches an ace, now bets, and gets several callers between him and the third-street raiser. If the third-street raiser now raises again, there is a good chance that he had a small three straight flush or at least a small three flush to start with, and that he now has four low cards and a four flush that may also have straight potential, with three cards yet to come. On the other hand, if the initial fourth-street bettor had caught just a small card instead of the ace, it would be conceivable for the strong player to raise with a hand that is not as powerful. In fact, a weaker hand would now be more likely.

When you can't actually put a person on a hand but have reduced his possible holdings to a limited number, you try to use mathematics to determine the chances of his having certain hands rather than others. Then you decide what kind of hand you must have to continue playing.

Sometimes you can use a mathematical procedure based on Bayes' Theorem to determine the chances that an opponent has one hand or another. After deciding on the kinds of hands your opponent would be betting in a particular situation, you determine the probability of your opponent holding each of those hands. Then you compare the probabilities.

Here's an example. Suppose a tight player starts with a six up, catches a blank on fourth street, and then catches an ace on fifth street. Now he bets. You hold a hidden pair of kings with two small cards up and are trying to determine whether you should call or fold. If a couple of aces were already exposed, especially on third street — meaning that it would be unlikely for your opponent to have two aces — you should continue on when he bets, since it is much more probable that you are against four low cards rather than three low cards and a pair of aces. Conversely, if the aces are all live and you think this is a likely card for your opponent to have in the hole, you should strongly consider folding, as you could be locked out of the high and your hand does not have two-way potential.

Knowing it is slightly more likely that your opponent has one kind of holding versus another does not always tell you how you should proceed in the play of your hand. Nevertheless, the more you know about the chances of an opponent having one hand rather than another when he bets or raises, the easier it is for you to decide whether to fold, call, or raise.

Here's another example. Suppose on third street that you have

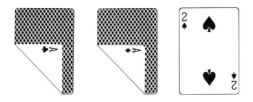

You raise, and an aggressive opponent behind you, who has a trey up, reraises. On fourth street, both you and your opponent pair your door cards, and he bets. If you think your opponent is equally as probable to have two other small cards in the hole as another trey, you should at least call. If you now catch a trey on fifth street and your opponent bets again after catching an eight, your play is to raise if you know this opponent would still bet if he had only a pair and four low cards. Since you have seen another trey, it is now much more mathematically likely that you have the best high hand, and you are a favorite to scoop the pot.

Finally, as this last example shows, you need to complement mathematical conclusions with what you know about a player. For example, some players almost always will raise with a hidden big pair in the hole and a small card up, trying to represent a strong low hand. If this type of player raises on third street and then catches small cards on fourth and fifth streets, he is less likely to have a quality low hand, and the chances that he has a high hand have increased. This would not be true if the raise came after several people with low cards already had limped in and if you know this player is reluctant to raise on big pairs in multiway pots. In this situation, the quality low hand is very likely.

Another factor in reading hands and deciding how to play your own hand is the number of players in the pot. People tend to play their hands much more straightforwardly in multiway pots. This is also true when several players are yet to act. So if a player bets in either of these situations (especially with several low cards showing), you can be quite sure that he's got a real hand.

Psychology

What I mean by the psychology of poker is getting into your opponents' heads, analyzing how they think, figuring out what they think you think, and even determining what they think you think they think. In this sense, the psychology of poker is an extension of reading opponents' hands, and it is also an extension of using deception in the way you play your own hand.

Here is an example. On third street, you have a low card up, are in a late position, have a hand of little value, and raise trying to steal the antes. You get reraised by a strong player, who was the bring-in (with a low card up) and who knows that you automatically would attempt to steal in this position. Since you know that he knows you automatically would try to steal, his reraise does not mean that he has a very good hand. Consequently, since your opponent might also be bluffing, the correct play may be for you to raise back and then to bet again on fourth and fifth streets as long as you catch decent cards.

This brings up another point. The above play works because you are against a strong player whose thinking makes sense. A weak player is a different story. Just as you can't put a weak player on a hand, you can't put him on a thought either.

Very sophisticated seven-card stud eight-or-better can go even beyond this third level. For example, an early-position player (who is high) catches a suited card on fourth street. He bets, and a strong player with two low cards showing calls. On fifth street, the player who is high catches a blank and bets again. His opponent, who thinks this player is probably on a flush draw (perhaps because he just called with the high upcard on third street), may now raise with only a small pair and three low cards. His opponent may realize this and raise back, trying to represent a strong hand. The initial raiser now may comprehend this possibility and call his opponent down. When the hand is over, assuming that the flush card does not come, if the initial raiser is actually against a flush draw, his calls will look fantastic to some opponents. Conversely, if it turns out that the first bettor really has a hand, the calls will look like a "sucker play."

At the expert level of seven-card stud eight-or better, the "skill" of trying to outwit your opponent sometimes can extend to so many levels that your judgment can begin to fail. However, in ordinary play against good players, you should think at least up to the third level. First, think about what your opponent has. Second, think about what your opponent thinks you have. And third, think about what your opponent thinks you think he has. Only when you are playing against weak players, who might not bother to think about what you have and who almost certainly don't think about what you think they have, does it not necessarily pay to go through such thought processes. Against all others, this is crucial to successful play, since deception is a big part of the game.

There are several other important ideas that play a major role in the psychology of poker. First, when an opponent bets in a situation where he is sure that you are going to call, he is not bluffing.

For example, suppose that a situation arises where you have been betting all the way, you bet again after all the cards are out, and a player raises you. It is rare to find an opponent who is capable of raising on the end as a bluff. This is particularly true in seven-card stud eight-or-better if your opponent is aware that you know you should just about always call, especially if it appears that you have a chance to escape with half the pot. Similarly, if you raise when all the cards are out and your opponent reraises, you usually should fold, unless your hand can beat some of the legitimate hands with which he might be raising or you have a reasonable chance to win half the pot. (But beware of the player who knows you are capable of these folds.)

However, folding is not necessarily correct on fifth or sixth street. Tough players will raise on these later streets if they have a mediocre hand that also has some potential to become a very strong hand. An example is a four-card low with a small pair. Those of you who fold when raised in these situations are giving up too much equity in the pot. This is especially true at the larger limits, where the games are usually tougher and these plays are common.

A corollary to the principle that we are discussing is that if your opponent bets when there appears to be a good chance that you will fold, he may very well be bluffing. What this means in practice is that if your opponent bets in a situation where he thinks he might be able to get away with a bluff, you have to give more consideration to calling him, even with a mediocre hand.

An example is when both you and your opponent appear to have four-card lows on fourth street but both catch blanks on fifth and sixth streets. If he now bets on the river, and he is the type of player who would try to pick up the pot with nothing, it may be correct to call or raise with a relatively weak hand.

In deciding whether to bet, it is equally important to consider what your opponent thinks you have. If your opponent suspects a strong hand, you should bluff more. (However, you should not bet a fair hand for value in this situation.)

An example of this is when you raise on fourth street with two small suited upcards and then catch a blank on fifth street. If you check on fifth street but bet again on sixth street when you catch a third small suited card, it is very hard for anyone going high to call with only a pair. So bet your small pairs in this spot.

Conversely, if you know your opponent suspects that you are weak, you should not try to bluff, as you will get caught. But you should bet your fair hands for value. As an example, if both you and your opponent checked on sixth street, you frequently can bet one big pair on the end for value, especially if it appears that your opponent is going low.

Varying your play and making an "incorrect" play intentionally are also part of the psychology of seven-card stud eight-or-better, because you are trying to affect the thinking of your opponents for future hands. On third street, for example, you occasionally may reraise a late-position player with a small card up, who may be on a steal, when you hold something like a rough three-card eight that does not have straight potential (especially if your hand is live). Assuming that your opponents see your hand in a showdown and it is obvious what you reraised with, they should be less inclined to steal against you in a similar situation. Also, you are taking advantage of the impression you created to get paid off later when you bet with a legitimate reraising hand.

Another example of this type of play is to throw in an extra raise early with a hand that doesn't really warrant it to give the *illusion of action*. For instance, on third street, you occasionally can reraise a high card smaller than an ace with a hand like

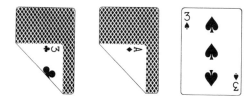

especially if you are going to play this holding anyway. This play costs only a fraction of a bet in mathematical expectation but gains you a tremendous amount in future action on subsequent hands.

There are also other ways to affect your opponents' play on future hands in stud eight-or-better. As an example, you may want to make what you think is a bad call if you believe this play will keep other players from running over you. If you find that you have been forced to throw away your hand on sixth street two or three times in a row, you must be prepared to call the next time with a hand that you normally wouldn't call with, even if it costs you several bets. This is because you can assume that your opponents have noticed your folding and are apt to try to "squeeze" you out.

Another less obvious situation where you should think of the future is to sometimes limp in early position on third street with a strong hand — such as a pair of aces and a small card, with one of the aces up. Then check again on fourth street and perhaps on fifth street, even if there was no raise on third street and even if you receive small cards. Not only may you catch someone stealing, but this check also might allow you to steal the pot yourself in a future hand when there has been almost no betting on the early rounds (especially when you catch a small card that pairs you). You can get away with a steal because you have shown your opponents that you are capable of checking a big hand twice. Thus someone with a mediocre hand may not call the double-sized fifth-street bet.

In general, you should evaluate any play you make on its merits alone, that is, on its expectation in a given situation. However, you occasionally might want to do something that is theoretically incorrect to create an impression for the future. Once you have opponents thinking one way, you can take advantage of that thinking later.

Finally, keep in mind that these types of plays will work against opponents who are good enough to try to take advantage of their new-found knowledge, but who are not good enough to realize that you know this and that they should therefore ignore it. In seven-card stud eight-or-better, as in all forms of poker, there seems to be a large group of players who like to "realize things." You must know how these people think and whether they are thinking only on the level that you are giving them credit for. If they think on a still higher level, you have to step up to that level.

Other Skills

Afterthought

As you have just seen, reading hands and psychology are extremely important aspects of seven-card stud eight-or-better. Put another way, this game is too complex to play by rote. If you always play a certain hand in a certain position a certain way, your game can use a lot of improvement. You must take into account your opponents, how the current hand has been played, how former hands were played, your opponents' perceptions of you, and so on. If you don't consider these things, you may be able to win, but you never will achieve expert status.

Many of the ideas in this section are most powerful against decent players — that is, players who play in predictable patterns and who are capable of realizing things when at the poker table. Against bad players, straightforward play is usually the best approach, and against extremely good players, these ideas probably can keep you only about even with them.

Finally, some players put too much emphasis on the topics just covered. They are certainly very important, but they are just some of the weapons that the expert has in his seven-card stud eight-or-better arsenal. To produce a top player, reading hands and psychology must be utilized in conjunction with all the other ideas and concepts that I have addressed.

Part Six

Questions and Answers

Questions and Answers

Introduction

A great deal of material has been covered in this book. However, for many people, reading and learning can be two different things. Consequently, to help you retain some of the more significant ideas, I have reiterated them in a question-and-answer format.

I suggest that after you have read and studied this text, you try to answer the following questions. You probably will want to go over them many times. In addition, I suggest that you cover the answer that immediately follows each question. Only look at the solution after you have answered the question to the best of your ability.

Also, I want to point out that what follows is not a substitute for the text. In fact, some of the ideas in the text are not contained here. But enough material is included so that after you have thoroughly digested the text, the questions should help keep your seven-card stud eight-or-better game sharp.

Finally, the questions and answers are organized by topics covered in the text, so you can easily return to the appropriate section for a fuller explanation.

Starting Hands

1. Other than rolled-up trips or three cards to a low straight flush, what is generally the best starting hand in stud eight-or-better?
   Two aces with a low card.

2. In what situation does two aces with a low card do best?
   In heads-up pots.

3. How should these hands be played?
   Either raise or reraise to thin out the field.

4. In what situation do three low cards to a straight do best?
   In a multiway pot when the cards needed to fill the open ends are very live and when this hand is not up against many other low hands.

5. How should you play three low cards to a straight or three low cards containing an ace?
   Very strongly, as long as your low cards are live.

6. What if your low cards are dead?
   Play these hands cautiously and be prepared to fold on fourth street if you catch bad and it appears that some of your opponents improve.

7. What should you do when one of these hands busts out?
   Be willing to get away from the hand quickly.

8. What happens once there are four people in?
   Three low cards to a straight does better than three low cards containing an ace that doesn't have straight possibilities.

121

9. How should you play when you start with three low cards to a straight and catch an ace?
   Aggressively.

10. Name a surprisingly good hand against a small number of opponents.
   6♥7♠8♣.

11. Why is the 6♥7♠8♣ so good in this situation?
   Against a high hand, it can escape for low as easily as a quality three-card low, but it is also easier for the 6♥7♠8♣ to make a high hand.

12. What is another good starting hand?
   The best high hand on board.

13. What is most important when playing this hand?
   That your cards are live.

14. What if you have the second-best high hand?
   Throw it away.

15. What is the only possible exception?
   When you have a two-card low as well.

16. What if several overcards are left to act and you have a big pair?
   Throw your hand away.

17. When is another time that big pairs can be costly?
   When several players with low cards showing have already entered the pot.

18. Why is that?
   You don't want to play against a low hand that has half the pot locked up and that also has a draw at the high side.

19. When is this likely to happen?
    When many low cards stay in.

20. What if an ace raises?
    You should throw your high pair away.

21. When you hold two kings, what would you like to be up against?
    A nine through a queen up.

22. What is next best?
    A deuce through an eight.

23. What about two kings against two opponents?
    You don't mind playing as long as neither has an ace up.

24. What about in most other spots?
    High pairs can be very tricky to play.

25. What is another of the better starting hands?
    Three high cards to a consecutive straight flush, as long as your cards are live.

26. What are two very dangerous hand categories?
    Small pairs with an ace kicker and small pairs with a small kicker.

27. If you play one of these hands, what would you prefer?
    That the side card to your pair be a straight flush card.

28. When playing one of these hands, why is it slightly better for your pair to be at least sixes?
    Because it is less likely that an opponent going for low will "accidentally" make a pair and beat you.

29. What if one of your opponents has a high pair?
    It won't matter whether your pair is sixes or lower.

30. How should you play one of these hands if you think you are up against a high pair?
    Throw your hand away for a raise. But if you can get in for a limp, you might want to take a card off.

31. Give an example of a typical razz hand.
    2♦6♥7♣.

32. Should you play these hands often?
    No. In fact, they frequently should be discarded, especially for a raise in games with a very high ante.

33. When might a typical razz hand become playable?
    When it is a little better than the example given, it does not cost too much, and your cards are live.

34. When is a three flush playable?
    When you are in a multiway pot with several hands against you that look as though they might be going high or you have two low cards. Also, your flush cards need to be very live.

35. If you have two low flush cards, is it beneficial for both of them to be in the hole?
    No. It is better to have one of them up.

36. Why?
    You will be disguised as a low hand and perhaps can drive out a low later if you make the flush.

37. When will you play a small pair with a medium or a large kicker?
    Only when everyone has gone out, you are in a steal position, and have a good chance to pick up the antes and bring-in.

38. What about higher three straights?
    These hands do very poorly.

39. What about medium high straights?
    They should just about never be played unless you are heads up against a high hand or perhaps in certain situations where your cards are completely live, you are against several weak players, and no one has raised or is likely to raise.

40. Is the present situation a determining factor on third street?
    Yes. It is often more important than the specific hand you are holding.

41. Since many starting hands are close in value, what is important?
    To fully assess the situation before deciding on the strength of your starting hand.

42. When do you raise on third street?
    You raise on third street only if you have a hand that plays better heads up, or if you have a hand that is very strong and several people are already in.

43. What if you have a typical playable three-card low and many players are yet to act?
    You probably should just "limp in."

44. What if other players are already in?
    You should call unless there has been a double raise.

45. When does an exception to just calling occur?
    When you are first in from a late position. Now you should raise.

Three of a Kind Wired

1. Suppose you have high trips and it appears as though a lot of players will be in the pot. How should you play?
    Play fast and stay to the end.

2. Does it matter much whether you are heads up or multiway?
    No.

3. What if your high trips are kings or queens?
    It will look as though you have only a big pair and are raising to limit the field.

4. What if your trips are between eights and jacks?
    You should play slower so that you can trap one or more high hands.

5. What about when your trips are small?
    Play it slow and let the high hands in.

6. What happens if your small trips appear to develop into a low hand?
    You can push it hard and jam the high hands.

Disguising Your Hand

1. What happens if you play against players who obviously have hands roughly equal to yours and you seldom raise?
   You give away too much information.

2. What happens when you do raise?
   Your opponents will be able to put you on a good low hand or a high hand.

3. Since a lot of bets are automatic according to how the cards fall, what will disguising your hand do for you?
   It will cause your opponents to make automatic bets that are incorrect.

4. Does disguising your hand always mean that you are going in the opposite direction than it appears?
   Not necessarily.

5) What else could it be?
   By disguising your hand, you might make your opponents think you have made a low hand when you actually have only four low cards and a pair.

6) What might a play like this do for you?
   It could make another low draw or a made weak low fold. In addition, it might allow you to value bet two pair on the end into a high hand.

Ante Stealing

1. When should you not attempt to steal the antes?
   When there are two or more low cards behind you.

2. When is it easiest to steal?
   When you have an ace up.

3. What is another good hand to steal with?
   A high card when there are one or two cards ranking nine or higher that still remain to act.

4. Example?
   You have a jack up, and there are a queen and a nine behind you. The player with the queen up usually will go out unless he has a pair of queens. The player with the nine up almost always will fold, even if he has two nines.

5. What if you are going to try to steal into low cards?
   You need an ace up or a medium low card, such as a six.

Getting
Reraised on a Semi-Steal

1. Suppose you have a medium small pair with a small kicker and you raise after most everyone has passed, hoping to steal the antes or to play heads up with the bring-in. You are raised back by an aggressive player with a low card that is smaller than your pair. Do you have the best hand?
   Usually.

2. What should you do?
   Raise back and play the hand aggressively.

3. On fourth street, if you catch a baby and your opponent catches anything from a nine on up, what may happen?
   You sometimes might win the pot right there.

4. What if you catch bad and your opponent catches small?
   You will have to make a tough decision, which might be to throw your hand away.

5. What if you both catch small cards?
   You probably will still want to lead.

6. What happens if you both catch bad?
   Your hand becomes stronger.

When an Ace Raises

1. Do you play many hands when an ace raises?
   No.

2. Should you throw away high pairs like kings and queens?
   Yes.

3. What do you need in order to play?
   Three very good low cards.

4. If you have a big pair and there is an ace behind you, what should you do?
   You should exercise caution. Be leery of raising or even playing your hand — especially if the ace is held by an aggressive player.

When the Bring-In Raises

1. What does it mean when the bring-in opens with a raise?
   He has a good hand, but not a great hand.

2. When the bring-in raises, what does he typically hold?
   Three small flush cards, three small straight cards, or a high pair in the hole.

3. Of these three possibilities, what is his most likely hand?
   A high pair in the hole, and he is trying to limit the field.

4. What is the exception?
   When the player is steaming.

General Strategy

1. What is a reasonable strategy to pursue?

   When the pot is still small in the early rounds, you should get out any time your hand does not look as though it is the best for one way or the other.

2. What if you don't do this?

   You may get trapped for a bigger bet and several raises on a later round.

3. What is the exception?

   When you have a two-way hand, it is usually worth chasing slightly better one-way hands.

4. What if no one catches anything that appears to make his hand?

   In this case, you may want to go a little further.

5. When else can you go a little further?

   When you are against players who tend not to jam unless they make cinches.

6. What about against more aggressive players who do jam a lot?

   You need to be careful about getting too involved.

7. How should you play when you hold a good hand?

   You should be a player who frequently will jam.

8. What will this do for you?

   It will make most of your opponents become cautious when playing against you, plus you will be able to control the size of the pot and how you want to play your hand.

9. What is an important skill in this game?
   The ability to size up what it will cost to see a hand through.

10. Why is this skill so important?
    Because instead of paying two or three bets to go to the river, as you would in most other games, it can easily end up costing you seven to ten bets.

11. Knowing whether someone plays tight or loose is not enough. What else do you need to know?
    How fast he plays and how often he jams the pots.

12. What type of hands do you want to play against those players who do play very fast?
    Two-way hands, hands that are well-disguised, and the bigger hands.

13. What about against players who are more passive?
    You can play a few additional hands.

14. What happens to one-way hands when playing heads up?
    They lose value.

15. If you are not a big favorite to win your half of the pot, what should you do?
    Throw your hand away, unless the pot is large.

16. Example?
    You hold 2♦4♣6♠7♥J♠ and are facing ?_? 5♣5♥5♦ or ?_? A♠4♦A♥. Throw your hand away.

17. What if you have a chance to scoop?
    It might be right to continue playing.

18. What if you hold a pair of queens and are against ? ? 4♦7♠2♠? You would play on, as it is unlikely that a straight or a bigger pair will be able to beat you.

19. What about one-way hands in multiway pots? They are also risky.

20. In a three-way pot, how much of a favorite to win your side do you need to be for a bet or raise to be correct? You need to be a 2-to-1 favorite.

21. Example? An opponent showing ? ? Q♠Q♣ bets. Another opponent calls with ? ? 5♥7♣. Your hand is 2♦A♠6♣4♠. In this situation, you have only a call. Even though you are a favorite to win your side, you are not a 2-to-1 favorite.

22. If it is still early in the hand and someone else is favored over you, no matter what the direction, what should you do? Fold.

23. When can you play a marginal hand? When you have a chance to win the whole pot.

24. Example? Suppose your first four cards are 5♦6♦7♥8♠. You can keep playing if it appears that you are up against a high pair and a better four-card low.

25. Suppose you have half the pot locked up but that is the only side you can win? Don't knock out other players.

26. When should you try to eliminate your opponents? When this will enable you to win the whole pot.

27. Example?

You have a big flush on fifth street. Your opponents show ?_?_2♦5♣Q♠ and ?_?_A♥5♠3♦. If the player holding the A♥5♠3♦ bets, you should raise in an attempt to get your other opponent to fold.

How Far Do You Go?

1. How do you play those hands you normally take further?
   With more strength earlier.

2. What about hands that you often fold early?
   With these hands, you want to put in as little money as possible.

3. Be specific.
   You will tend to go further with hands like three small straight cards — particularly if the cards are suited — and two aces with a small card.

4. When should you fold two aces with a small card?
   When someone who raised with a high card up pairs his door card.

5. When should you consider folding a small three straight that does not improve?
   When someone who started with a small card up catches a suited baby on fourth street.

Fourth Street

1. What is one of the biggest mistakes you can make in stud eight-or-better?

To call a bet on fourth street when you catch a bad card and your opponents catch a second good low card.

2. Why is this such a big error?

Because that second low card must help your opponent in one way or another.

3. Suppose you are high and a couple of your opponents catch another low card that is close in rank to their third-street cards. What should you do?

Fold.

4. Why?

Because you might be against more than one four straight, as well as a low draw.

5. What if the pot is heads up, your opponent catches another low card close in rank to his upcard, and you hold a high hand?

You can take a card off.

6. In a multiway pot, suppose you hold three low cards, there is a high hand against you, and someone has raised with a wheel card up, showing early strength. That player then catches a small card close in rank to his door card, and you catch a seven or an eight. What should you do?

Unless you also have a straight or a flush draw, you almost always should fold.

7. Example?

You have 7♣6♣3♥2♦, and an opponent has a hand like ? ? 5♠3♦. The high bets, and your opponent holding the low hand now raises. You must muck your hand.

8. Suppose you start with a small three straight and catch close to perfect. What should you do?

Bet the hand for value.

9. If you are playing for a high hand, and on fourth street your cards start to fall a bit dead, what should you do?

It is probably best to get out when you are looking at an opponent with two low cards.

10. Why?

Your hand is now a playing loser, as opposed to a percentage loser.

11. What should you do if your cards stay live, but you catch bad on fourth street and are against two opponents who have both caught low straight cards to go along with their low third-street cards?

You probably should get out.

12. What if one opponent caught good and the other caught bad?

You might want to bet, raise, or check-raise and try to force the low hand that caught bad to fold.

13. What if your opponent catches another low card that is a straight flush card?

It is usually best to go out, unless you have improved a great deal or have a hand that can win on its own.

14. What is one of the problems with continuing to play?
> You won't know whether your opponent is going high or low.

15. What if your opponent catches a suited ace?
> The situation is often similar.

16. What if you are playing the high hand and a player who stood a raise going in catches a live ace on fourth street?
> It is usually best to give up if your opponent bets.

17. If you start with a low hand and catch bad, what should you do?
> Usually get out.

18. What are the exceptions?
> 1. The pot is extremely large.
> 2. You started with a premium hand. Or
> 3. Everyone catches bad.

19. What else must you do on fourth street?
> Think about how to set up your play of the hand.

20. What typically happens when it is heads up?
> The player with the best hand will be betting.

21. What does it mean when a player who showed strength on third street catches good but doesn't bet after he is checked to?
> Most of the time, failing to bet indicates that the fourth-street card did not help him.

22. What must you do if you have the best high hand?
> You must decide whether to narrow the field.

23. What if you don't think you can narrow the field?
    You don't want to take charge and put a lot of money in the pot.

24. What is one reason for sometimes not playing fast?
    To determine where the strength is.

25. Why is this important?
    Determining where the strength is will enable you to make better decisions later in the hand.

26. When should you consider disguising your hand?
    When you have a quality low hand or a hidden high hand, such as small trips or aces in the hole with two small cards.

Check-Raising on
Fourth and Fifth Streets

1. What is one of the key tools that an expert player will use?
Check-raising.

2. Why can check-raising be used a lot in this game?
Because hands are often disguised, plus it becomes obvious as to who will do the betting.

3. Be specific.
Usually the player who is low and catches another low card will bet, or the high hand will bet if his opponent busts out.

4. What is another reason to try for a check-raise?
Giving a free card when trying to check-raise is not so terrible in this game, since most opponents will call your bet anyway.

5. What does the check-raise enable you to do?
To gain a double bet, as well as to frequently knock out players who are going the same way as you are.

6. Example?
You have two aces but also have low possibilities developing. If your check-raise knocks out another high hand, or if you can knock out a low hand and play against a weaker high hand where you have a chance to make low if he should outdraw you for high, you have accomplished a lot.

Fifth Street

1. Suppose on fourth street that you have a good four-card low, which is also a four straight or four flush. If you bust out on fifth street but your hand is still live, should you bet?

    If you still have a good chance to scoop, you should bet.

2. Suppose you are playing heads up, you are going high, and your opponent is going low. What should you do?

    Bet, unless he has three low cards up.

3. What if he has three low cards up?

    Either check and call or check and fold, depending on the three low cards and on exactly how strong your hand is.

4. What if you are against a possible good four-card low, which also may be a straight draw?

    You should be inclined to check.

5. What if you think your opponent may have three low cards, a pair, and a bust card?

    You should bet and be willing to call a raise if it comes.

6. You are in a three-way pot, and one of your opponents is going the same direction as you are. What should you do if you have the best hand for your direction?

    Try to eliminate the player going the opposite way.

7. Example?

On fifth street, you have 2♣3♦5♥K♠A♦. Your opponent who appears to be going low is in the middle with ? ? 4♠7♥10♣, and the player going high has ? ? Q♥9♠5♦. You may want to try to check-raise the player going high. Notice that the player going high may fold, since he might think you have made aces.

8. What if someone who appears to be going low just checks and calls?

It is almost certain that he has a low draw but doesn't have a good straight or flush draw to go along with it.

9. What is critical for you to do on fifth street?

To mix up your play a fair amount.

10. Example?

With a busted low hand and a high card on fifth street, you may want to check-raise or even jam to disguise your hand.

11. Suppose you have made an eight or a rough seven for low, and you are looking at a hand like ? ? A♠2♦3♣ or ? ? 3♦4♣5♥. What should you do?

Throw your hand away.

12. What happens to a high hand when someone makes a low on fifth street?

It becomes very weak. You must consider folding.

13. In what circumstances do you play on?

If it is heads up and the pot is fairly large, or if you are not likely to get scooped.

14. Example?

Continue playing against ? ? 2♠4♣7♥, but fold against ? ? 3♦4♠5♣.

15. What if you have a big pair and your opponent's board is something in between the two hands just given?

You should consider how live the possible straight or flush cards are for your opponent.

16. What if your opponent's third low upcard is an ace?

You generally should go out.

17. When do the high hands do well?

When the low hands have busted out by fifth street.

18. What if you have any doubt as to whether you should continue playing or fold on fifth street?

You should fold, unless you have a good chance for half the pot or a decent chance for all of it.

Sixth Street

1. Do you ever fold on sixth street?
   Yes. You frequently should do so.

2. Why?
   Because one or more of your opponents can catch a card that might mean you are drawing dead, plus there may be a bet and a raise.

3. Be specific.
   When there is a lot of betting and raising on sixth street, the pot is virtually certain to be split. You will not be getting the odds you need to attempt to draw out on the high end when you have only two pair.

4. What does this mean?
   It generally means that the only time you should try to catch is when you have a lot of outs — such as when you hold a good low draw, a flush draw, or trips — and you are getting the proper odds.

Seventh Street

1. Even though it is likely that your opponents were drawing to beat you, what should you do on seventh street if you happened to have the best hand on sixth street?

Usually bet anyway.

2. What is the exception?

If you have a made low hand and are against a high hand and one or more opponents who were drawing to a better low.

3. What if you have the best low hand and are against other players with made low hands who are likely to pay off?

Then, of course, you should bet or raise into them.

4. What if you have a high hand, there are low hands against you, and a split pot is certain (as long as one of the low hands hasn't improved to a straight, a flush, or something better, and it is likely that one or more of these draws is out)?

You should check and call.

5. What if you have a high hand and there are two or three players in the pot who look as though they will call with weaker high hands?

You should lead on the end.

6. Suppose you miss a low draw but make a pair, perhaps even a small pair. A player who has been betting most of the way bets again, and it appears that he has a low hand. What should you do?

Call. You might even win the whole pot if he is bluffing.

7. What else might you do in this spot?

Consider raising if there is some chance that you can knock out a high hand.

8. Suppose you have a high two pair and are against an opponent who shows three low cards but who probably has not made his low hand by sixth street. What should you do?

Bet on the river. If your opponent makes two pair, he normally will pay off your bet.

9. Suppose you have a big pair in the hole, plus some small cards up, and you are against an opponent who seems to also have a big pair. He has been calling you down, although his pair doesn't appear as large as yours. What do you do if your opponent checks to you on the river?

Bet your one big pair for value.

10. Suppose you are going for low but make two pair, and someone holding an obvious big pair checks to you. What should you do?

Bet your hand for value.

11. Can you bluff a high hand if it appears that there is a reasonable chance you are going low?

No.

12. Are there situations where you should bet as a bluff?

Yes.

13. Example?

Suppose you have 7♠6♥4♣3♦J♠10♥2♠ and are against one opponent who shows ? ? 3♦7♣K♠Q♥? . Notice that you are beat for high and also might be beat for low. Nevertheless, betting is correct.

Position

1. What position is most advantageous?
   Being last to act.

2. Why is it helpful for the high hand to be on your left?
   This gives you an opportunity to know how expensive it will be to see the next card.

3. What are two advantages of positional strength?
   Positional strength gives you the opportunity to bluff or squeeze out an opponent, plus it allows you to see how many bets it will be to you.

4. If your position is poor and there are aggressive players behind you, how should you play your marginal hands?
   You should give up on many of them.

5. What if you are last to act and it is only one bet to you?
   Many of these marginal holdings can be played.

Playing the High Hands

1. What must you be sure of when you play a high hand?
   That it is the best high hand.

2. If you are the high hand and are playing heads up against a low hand who has caught two more low cards by fifth street, what should you do?
   You frequently should fold, unless you have improved to at least two pair.

3. What do you do if you have improved to two pair?
   Usually go to the river and pay it off.

4. When should you play the high hands strongly?
   When there are other high cards out.

5. What are you hoping to accomplish?
   To trap the second- and third-best high hands, and to drive out the low hands.

6. Suppose you are playing a high hand heads up against a probable low hand that has a wheel card showing on third street and then catches an ace on fourth street. What should you do?
   Usually fold immediately.

7. Can you ever call in this spot?
   Yes. You sometimes can make a "crying call" and then must be prepared to fold on fifth street if your opponent catches anything that looks as though it could be trouble or if your hand falls slightly dead.

8. What if your opponent, who appears to be going low, pairs his door card on fourth street?

    You should fold.

9. How should you play when there could be two low hands out against you?

    You should try to avoid putting in a lot of money early with a high hand.

10. When is a good time to push a high hand?

    When you are against another high hand that is not as good as yours and a low draw.

Bluffing

1. When you bluff, what are you usually trying to do?
   To knock out another hand that you don't want to contest your way.

2. When might you bluff trying to win the whole pot?
   When you are playing heads up, if you miss on the end, think your lone opponent might also have missed on the end, and don't think he will call with a small pair, then you may bluff trying to win the whole pot.

3. Suppose it looks as though you were drawing at a flush, or it is obvious that you had two pair or trips and were jammed in on sixth street by what appears to be a straight and a lock low. On the river, the low bets. What can you do?
   Bluff with a raise.

4. If the player with the straight calls and the low reraises, what can you do?
   Raise again, and you might convince the holder of the better high hand that he is beat.

5. When making this play, what should you keep in mind?
   That you must commit a lot of chips, plus you'll have to be very cautious of whom you use this play against.

Slow-Playing

1. When might you slow-play?

   When you have a low hand that is not likely to be beat.

2. Example?

   You have 4♦5♥6♠A♣2♣ and are in a multiway pot. There are no other completed lows, several treys are dead, and no one has what could be a wheel draw. Since someone will have to catch perfect twice to beat you, you may want to slow-play.

3. What if you have a high draw to go along with your low hand?

   You may want to play hard and fast.

4. Example?

   If all the treys were live in the example just given, you probably would not want to slow-play your hand.

5. What if you hold a high hand?

   You should not slow-play, because you have a chance to win the whole pot.

6. But what if you hold a very big high hand that is not likely to be beat, and it is obvious that a low has been made?

   In this situation, it becomes correct to slow-play.

Knowing Your Opponents

1. When a tight player comes in with a raise, what does it usually mean?

    He has a high hand or a very strong low hand.

2. What should you do in this situation?

    You should throw away hands that look fairly good under ordinary circumstances, as now they are not even marginal.

3. What is the exception?

    If you know a player extremely well and are fairly certain of what his hand is.

4. How do seven-card stud players typically play?

    They tend to play high hands strongly and stay with them longer. That is, they will be aggressive with big pairs and cautious with low hands.

5. What about a razz player?

    He will do just the opposite.

6. What about the top eight-or-better players?

    They have a good mix to their games.

7. There are many players who tend to play more one way than the other. Give an example.

    When the table is full, some players generally will play only quality low hands that are often three straights.

8. How should you play when one of these players catches perfect on fourth street?

    You should not give him any action.

9. What if this player now checks?
   He is probably paired.

10. What if he bets out into several players or raises?
    He has caught good.

Raising Aggressively

1. Why do you occasionally raise?
   To set up a play, to disguise your hand, or to knock someone out.

2. Do you ever raise to get a free card?
   Only very rarely.

3. Why is this?
   Because many of your opponents will raise back, plus the free cards that you get won't have the potential, as they do in many other games, to make a big disguised hand.

4. Does raising gain you valuable information?
   Not usually.

5. Why not?
   If an opponent has a playable hand, he generally will hang on, whether you raise or not.

6. What typically might happen if you raise?
   You might find yourself calling a reraise and thus being forced to play to the end.

The Toughest Decision of All

1. What is the toughest decision you'll have to make in stud eight-or-better?

Whether to fold on a late street — after you have already put a lot of money in the pot — when an opponent catches a card that could make you the second-best low hand or could even cause you to be drawing dead.

2. What should you normally do in this situation?
Bet your hand.

3. What if this player now raises?
If he is a player without much imagination, it's best to throw away your hand, unless you have a quality draw to beat him.

4. What if he is a player with a lot of imagination?
Then you may want to continue playing.

Staying to the End

1. When should you usually stay to the end with a good low draw?
   When you are trying to make the best low or a hand that has a reasonable chance of being the best low but is also an inside straight draw or better.

2. When is it correct to throw away these hands?
   When your hand is not very live, the pot odds you are getting are not very good, or the chances are high that you'll make your hand but it will not be the best hand.

Pairing the Door Card

1. If you are going high, pair your door card, and make trips, what should you do?

    Bet out and continue betting most of the way through the hand.

2. What if someone raises?

    You should reraise, unless it looks as though there is a good chance that you are beat.

3. What situation might indicate that you are beat?

    If the raise occurs in heads-up play and you are looking at three low cards.

4. If you are low and pair your door card, what might this enable you to do?

    To disguise your hand and perhaps to bluff a little.

5. What will the high card typically do in this situation?

    He generally will take one more card off. If you catch another low card (on fifth street), he usually will give up unless he has made at least two pair.

6. What if you catch a bust card on fifth street?

    The high hand almost always will play on, so you need trips or at least two pair to bet.

7. What is the bad part about pairing your door card when you have a low card up?

    You probably will be first to act the rest of the way.

8. What if you are up against other low hands and you pair your small door card?

> This puts you at a definite disadvantage.

9. If you pair your low door card and make trips, how should you play your hand?

> You should play it as though you had made big trips.

10. What if you have a big pair in the hole?

> You should usually bet your hand all the way through.

11. When your opponent pairs his small door card, what does he usually have?

> Three low cards with a pair or two big pair. It is less likely that he has trips.

12. But if he is a tight player and continues to play very aggressively, what is his hand?

> He usually has trips or the two big pair.

13. In a multiway pot, what if the player on your immediate right pairs his door card?

> It puts you at a significant disadvantage during the hand.

14. Under what circumstances is this especially true?

> If this opponent is an aggressive player, or if he is a weak player who is liable to keep betting without the best hand just because he is high.

15. Since you might find yourself jammed in on a later round, what is necessary for you to continue playing?

> You must have helped your hand considerably on both fourth street and fifth street.

Keeping Track of the Cards

1. Do you need to keep track of the cards?
   Yes, especially the low cards.

2. Why?
   Many situations will develop where you need one or two cards to make your hand, or you will need to know how live certain cards are to determine whether it is likely that an opponent will have a particular hand.

3. Example?
   Suppose you have a six-high straight and are worried that an opponent might have a split with you or a wheel. Remembering the cards will have a large effect on whether you should jam or not.

4. What about the cards you don't see?
   You can deduce a great deal about them.

5. Example?
   Suppose that someone starts with a low card up, meaning that he probably is going low. If he folds after catching another low card, such as a deuce — which might have given him four good cards — you can conclude that two deuces are gone.

Scare Cards

1. Do scare cards help your hand in stud eight-or-better?
   Usually.

2. Why?
   Because hands in eight-or-better are less disguised than they
   are in high-only seven-card stud.

3. Be specific.
   Hands in stud eight-or-better are more likely to be built
   around the upcard.

An Expert Play

1. Suppose you start with four low cards and are playing heads up against a mediocre high hand, such as a high pair. You believe your opponent has put you on these four low cards. What can you do if you catch a big card on fifth street?
  You can check-raise.

2. What will most players think?
  They will believe you have a high hand.

3. What if your opponent thinks you have made trips or two big pair?
  He might throw his hand away.

4. What if he calls and you make an open pair?
  You can bet out, and there is a good chance that he will fold.

5. What if you catch another low card?
  Your opponent probably will continue to play, although he may go out if he fears a straight.

6. What if you catch a garbage card?
  You should check, and your opponent will put you on a four-card straight and will bet.

7. What should you now do?
  Check-raise him again.

8. What is likely to happen if your opponent calls?
  He probably won't pay it off on the river.

9. What if your opponent won't bet on sixth street?
  Then this play won't work.

Another Good Play

1. In a three-way pot on fifth street, suppose one player has an obvious high hand, you have four low cards and make a small open pair, and the third player appears to have made his low. What should you do?

You should check. The high hand probably will check also, the low hand will bet, and now you can check-raise.

2. What will the high hand think you have?

At least two pair and probably trips.

3. What generally will happen?

Your raise usually will knock out the high hand, enabling you to play heads up against the low hand.

4. What if the low hand goes to three bets?

There is a good chance that he has an additional draw with his low hand.

5. What might happen if you make your low hand?

You may scoop the pot if your small pair holds up for high.

6. What if you suspect that you have just been a victim of this play?

When someone raises or check-raises into you with an open pair, you can't continue playing with a high pair, since the low is already made.

Reading Hands

1. What is the most common way to read hands?

Analyze the meaning of an opponent's check, bet, or raise, and then consider the plays he has made throughout the hand, along with the exposed cards, to come to a determination about his hand.

2. Is it a mistake to put an opponent on a hand early and to stick with your initial conclusion?

Yes.

3. On third street, suppose that you raise with a high card up and an opponent showing a small card calls your raise. On fourth street, he catches another small card close in rank to his upcard and bets after you check. You call, and on fifth street you both catch blanks. When you check, he also checks. What is a likely hand for him to have?

A three-card low with a small pair.

4. What if your opponent catches another low card on sixth street that appears to possibly give him a small straight?

You should not fold.

5. What if he catches a blank on sixth street?

You should bet and then probably bet again on the river if you make two pair.

6. But if he catches good on sixth street, how should you play on the river?

You should check and call, since you still have a good shot at the high half of the pot (or you might even scoop the whole pot).

7. What if you cannot beat a small pair?

You may want to bet, since there is some chance that you can pick up the pot if your opponent has missed his low.

8. In practice, what should you try to determine?

Whether your opponent has a bad hand, a mediocre hand, a good hand, or a great hand.

9. If an opponent bets on the end, what type of hand is he unlikely to have?

A mediocre hand.

10. What is a complementary way to read hands?

To work backward.

11. If someone with a small card up cold calls a raise and a reraise by a king and a small card, catches medium-sized cards higher than an eight on fourth and fifth streets, but is able to raise on sixth street, what is his probable hand?

A rolled-up set. It does not seem possible that he would have gone this far with something like a small three straight.

12. Suppose on sixth street that a player who called a raise on third street has ? ? 2♣Q♣6♠10♥. Someone with a king in the door and a small pair on board bets; another player who caught an ace on sixth street and who has two other small cards up, both lower than a six, raises; and now this person calls the raise. Does he have just a draw to a six?

No, even though it is likely that he started with three small cards.

13. Why is that?

Given the cards showing in his opponents' hands, he may have only a small chance of winning just half the pot.

14. What does this player figure to have?

   At least a gut-shot straight draw, but more likely a flush draw as well.

15. When you have reduced your opponent's possible hands to a limited number, what do you use to determine what he probably holds?

   Mathematics.

16. Suppose a tight player starts with a six up, catches a blank on fourth street, and then catches an ace on fifth street. Now he bets. You hold a hidden pair of kings with two small cards up and are trying to determine whether you should call or fold. If a couple of aces already were exposed, especially on third street, what should you do?

   You should continue on when be bets.

17. Why is this correct?

   Because it is much more probable that you are against four low cards rather than three low cards and a pair of aces.

18. What if the aces are all live and you think this is a likely card for your opponent to have in the hole?

   You should strongly consider folding.

19. Why?

   Because you could be locked out of the high and your hand does not have two-way potential.

20. Suppose you start with A♣A♦2♠. You raise, and an aggressive opponent behind you, who has a trey up, reraises. On fourth street, both you and your opponent pair your door cards, and he bets. What should you do?

> If you think your opponent is equally as probable to have two other small cards in the hole as another trey, you should at least call.

21. If you now catch a trey on fifth street and your opponent bets again after catching an eight, what is your play?

> Your play is to raise if you know this opponent would bet again if he had only a pair and four low cards.

22. What is another factor in reading hands and deciding how to play your own hand?

> The number of players in the pot.

23. How do players tend to play their hands in multiway pots?

> Much more straightforwardly.

24. When else do they play in a more straightforward manner?

> When several players are yet to act.

Psychology

1. What is meant by "the psychology of poker"?

Getting into your opponents' heads, analyzing how they think, figuring out what they think you think, and even determining what they think you think they think.

2. Suppose on third street that you have a low card up, are in a late position, have a hand of little value, and raise trying to steal the antes. You are reraised by a strong opponent, who was the bring-in and who knows that you automatically would try to steal in this position. What may be the correct play for you?

To raise back and then to bet on fourth and fifth streets.

3. Would you make this play against a weak player?

No.

4. When an opponent bets in a situation where he is sure that you are going to call, is he bluffing?

No.

5. Example?

If you have been betting all the way, you bet again after all the cards are out, and a player raises you, he is not bluffing.

6. Do players generally raise as a bluff on fifth or sixth street?

No, tough players will raise on these later streets with a mediocre hand that has some potential to become a very strong hand.

7. When might your opponent be bluffing?

When there appears to be a good chance that you will fold.

8. Give an example.

Both you and your opponent appear to have four low cards on fourth street but both catch blanks on fifth and sixth streets. If he now bets on the river, and he is the type of player who would try to pick up the pot with nothing, it may be correct to call or raise with a relatively weak hand.

9. In deciding whether to bet, what else is important to consider?

What your opponent thinks you have.

10. If your opponent suspects a strong hand, what should you do?

Bluff more.

11. Give an example.

Suppose you raise on fourth street with two small suited upcards and catch a blank on fifth street. If you check on fifth street but bet again on sixth street when you catch a third small suited card, it is very hard for anyone going high to call with only one pair. So bet your small pairs in this spot.

12. What if your opponent suspects that you are weak?

Don't try to bluff, but bet your fair hands for value.

13. Example?

If both you and your opponent checked on sixth street, you frequently can bet one big pair on the end for value, especially if it appears that your opponent is going low.

14. Should you ever intentionally make an incorrect play?

Yes.

15) Why?

Because you are trying to affect the thinking of your opponents for future hands.

16. Give an example.

On third street, you occasionally reraise a late-position player with a small card up, who may be on a steal, when you hold something like a rough three-card eight that does not have straight potential (especially if your hand is live).

17. What type of players do these kinds of plays work well against?

Players who are good enough to try to take advantage of their new-found knowledge, but who are not good enough to realize that you know this.

Questions and Answers

Afterthought

Again, these questions are not designed as a replacement for the material in the text. Their purpose is to help keep you sharp between full readings of *High-Low-Split Poker Seven-Card Stud Eight-or-Better For Advanced Players*. I recommend that when you believe you have become a winning seven-card stud eight-or-better player that you reread the text material every other month and review the questions about once a week. Also, remember to cover the answers and to think through those questions that you have trouble with. In addition, attempt to relate the questions to recent hands that you have played, and try to determine which concepts were the correct ones to apply.

Another thing to keep in mind, as has been mentioned several times in this book, is that seven-card stud eight-or-better is not that simple. This means that you should be a student for life. It takes a long time to become an expert player. That is why continuous review of these questions (and the rest of the material in this book) is an absolute necessity.

Conclusion

To sit in a seven-card stud eight-or-better game, especially at the higher limits, you'd better play well, because this game does not get the drop-in traffic that some other forms of poker usually get. Almost all of your opponents in stud eight-or-better will be veterans. So just playing tight won't do the trick, as many of your adversaries will play approximately the same selection of hands that you do. To be successful, you must be an expert, particularly on the later streets.

But the game can be beat. In fact, if you play very well, you can expect to do very well, since many of your opponents will be too timid on the later streets and won't take advantage of the opportunities that are presented to them. Others will be too aggressive and will jam in spots where they don't have the best of it. You not only need to do these things correctly, but also must be able to adjust to the opponents that you are playing against.

Perhaps the least known — and most controversial — advice given in this book has to do with bluffing in an attempt to win half the pot. In fact, I suspect that some readers will believe that I recommend bluffing too much in these situations. Rest assured that this is not the case. I know from a theoretical point of view, plus from much practical experience, that these plays are correct and are part of a strong winning strategy.

I expect this book to have a major impact, not only on those of you who read and study it, but also on the games themselves. In general, there will begin to be more tough players around, meaning that some games will be tougher to beat. On the other hand, I also expect that this text will be a significant contributor to the future growth of seven-card stud eight-or-better. Consequently, there will be more games around, and the expert player thus will have more games from which to choose. I therefore expect that in the long run, this book will benefit those of you who make a commitment to studying the ideas it contains.

Finally, serious stud eight-or-better players who ignore the contents of this book will be left behind. I believe this is true even if you currently are having a successful run at the game. This should give you an idea of how strong the strategies and concepts really are in *High-Low Split Poker Seven-Card Stud Eight-or-Better For Advanced Players.*

RAY ZEE

High-Low-Split Poker
Omaha
Eight-or-Better

For Advanced Players

One of the foremost poker players/writers in America shows how a good Omaha eight-or-better player can become a great Omaha eight-or-better player.

Introduction

Omaha high-low split eight-or-better is a game of false reputations, and opinions differ. Some people will tell you that this is the action game, the game of numerous combinations, and the form of poker that requires the most skill. Others will say that this is the game where you are correct to play exceedingly tight, there is no skill, and you should play with absolutely no imagination.

But neither opinion accurately describes Omaha high-low split eight-or-better. At the lower limits, where many people play poorly and some of the games are extremely loose, just playing tight will make money. However, this is not the case at the higher limits, and skillful players have learned that numerous poker skills are required to be a consistent winner.

What follows is a very strong winning approach, no matter what your limit might be. The text contains a basic strategy section that is applicable to the low-limit games and should enable you to win consistently, as long as the competition is not tough. However, if you wish to be successful at the higher limits, you need to study the entire text. The basic strategy section alone will not be enough.

Recently, this game has been growing in popularity, especially among players who are fairly new to poker. This might be because they have not yet discovered hold 'em or stud. More experienced players who already have a favorite game seem reluctant to try Omaha eight-or-better. Nevertheless, because of the game's increasing popularity, it is generally available in most major locations where poker is played.

This book, like the other books in the *For Advanced Players* series, basically teaches a tight but aggressive approach. However, at times I will recommend that you play more hands than you might expect, but I also will advise you to throw away other hands in some situations that many of your opponents will play, partly

177

because this book is written for advanced players. If you are new to this game — even if you are very experienced at another form of poker — and you choose to play at the higher limits, you probably will want to play more conservatively than what the text indicates. However, with experience, you can completely follow the guidelines. If you wish to play in the small games, it won't be necessary to tighten up, since conservative play is recommended at these limits.

In most forms of poker, the players tend to get tougher as you move to a higher limit, because successful players generally move up. Although there are exceptions, the high-limit Omaha eight-or-better games are often extremely different from the smaller games. You will need many more poker skills to win at the higher limits, and some of the ideas that apply to these games are irrelevant at the lower limits. In other words, you should not jump into a high-limit game after a quick reading of this book. If you do so, you will, as they say, "get killed." Players *are* better as the limits go up, and you'd better be ready for them.

As noted, the Omaha eight-or-better basic strategy section should provide enough information for you to be successful in the smaller games. Eventually, however, you may want to take some shots at the bigger games, where players are capable of thinking on many different levels. The only way you can guarantee your success at the higher limits is to absorb the information in this book, plus accumulate a great deal of experience and do some hard thinking about the game.

Finally, some players whom I have played against over the years in the high-stakes games, and whom you eventually may have the opportunity to play against, are Tom Hufnagle — an expert who's fun to play with; Lee Wosk — a Colorado player who can play with the best of them; Pierre — a Reno player who always plays his best; Berry Johnston — a former world champion, a first-class guy, and someone who can take a good ribbing when he's stuck in a game; Mike Sexton — who gets the job done; and Jack Keller — another former world champion who exemplifies aggressiveness.

Using This Book

This book will require you to do a lot of thinking. I recommend that the whole text be read first, then you can return to those sections that require more study.

Keep in mind that this book is for advanced players. If you are new to Omaha eight-or-better and wish to play in the higher limits, it is best to play more conservatively than what is recommended. As you gain experience, you will begin to see where it is appropriate to try out the plays that are discussed. If you play in the smaller limits, you should try to play as recommended for those games.

I also advise that you not jump right into a high-limit game. Even though the strategies in this book will win their share at the higher limits, especially if the opposition is not too tough, it is imperative to get some experience first.

In addition, it is very important in Omaha eight-or-better to recognize when you have the best hand. This can be difficult at times. A common beginner's mistake is to play a hand that appears to be good but is not really worthwhile, especially once the flop comes. You should pay strict attention to when hands are playable and when they are not. Failing to do so can be very expensive.

The Omaha section of *High-Low-Split Poker* was written with two model games in mind. The first is the low-limit game, defined as $10-$20 and below; the second is the high-limit game, classified as $50-$100 and above. Both games have the same structure and require a small blind to the left of the button and a large blind two positions to the left of the button. Bets and raises before the flop and on the flop are equal to the large blind, and bets and raises on the last two rounds are double the amount of the large blind. These two games are different, because the skill level of many players who populate the high-limit games is much more sophisticated than that of typical players who compete in the lower limits. This requires many changes in strategy.

Because Omaha is a form of hold 'em and many advanced strategies for hold 'em will apply in this game, every serious Omaha player should read *Hold 'em Poker For Advanced Players* by David Sklansky and Mason Malmuth. I also recommend that you read *The Theory of Poker* by David Sklansky, which covers many of the general concepts essential to beating Omaha eight-or-better. In fact, fully comprehending the more specific Omaha eight-or-better ideas presented in this book will be difficult without first reading *The Theory of Poker*.

Why Play
Omaha Eight-or-Better

As poker games go, Omaha eight-or-better is not the most exciting. At the lower limits, playing correctly can be boring. At the higher limits, even though the game now requires a lot of skill, it is still not as complex as Texas hold 'em or seven-card stud.

This seems to imply that the profit potential is not as high in this game as it is in some other forms of poker; that you won't have the opportunities to make many expert plays, which are necessary to be a big winner; and that you won't enjoy this game to the degree that you can enjoy either Texas hold 'em or seven-card stud.

While there is some truth to these statements, there is one overriding exception. It has to do with the fact that many of your opponents will not perceive this game as just described. They believe Omaha eight-or-better is incredibly complex, often citing that an Omaha hand contains six hold 'em hands as opposed to only one. They also believe the strategy options are virtually endless.

These beliefs enable your opponents to justify playing too many hands and to play some hands very imaginatively. They get trapped in pots that they have no business being in, and they don't understand the correct value of many hands they play. In other words, the games are frequently very good.

Even so, your poker skills are still required, especially at the higher limits. Becoming an expert at this form of poker will enable you to improve your game, no matter what other form of poker you also may be interested in playing.

Incidentally, new players with little skill are attracted to this game. When someone begins to play poker, he quickly hears that Omaha, in its different forms, is the game of the future. This attracts him to the Omaha eight-or-better table, since high-only limit Omaha is not spread as frequently. After a couple of months, he often abandons this game for either Texas hold 'em or seven-card stud. But there always seems to be someone new to take his place, which is another reason that these games are good.

In conclusion, Omaha eight-or-better can be a rewarding game, though at times it also can be very frustrating. It isn't as widely spread as Texas hold 'em or seven-card stud, but most major cardrooms now offer it. If you become an expert at this game, you can expect to do very well. But remember that you won't become a champion overnight. It will require lots of study and playing experience.

Part One

Basic Strategy

Basic Strategy

Introduction

In the low-limit Omaha eight-or-better games, you must play tight, because a lot of players in these games play poorly and very loosely. This creates many multiway pots, making it difficult for a good player to manipulate a weaker hand into a winner.

One of the interesting things about low-limit Omaha eight-or-better is that a poor player can go for a long period of time before he realizes how badly he plays. This is because poor players are often in the pot with other poor players, and they end up pushing their chips back and forth. If one of them runs good for a while, he may think he is an expert. Eventually, however, he will become a loser.

Although playing tight is very important, it is not all that's necessary to be a consistent winner at this game. Omaha eight-or-better is not completely cut-and-dried. You still need a good understanding of the game, even if your opponents are weak.

General Concepts

When playing in the lower limits, which I've defined as $10-$20 and below, there are two kinds of games. The first type is a game in which people are playing too loosely, especially after the flop; the second is a game where the players generally know what they are doing. In the first type of game, where people play too loosely, the main error is that many players draw to hands — especially low hands — that are not the nuts. If you find yourself in a game like this, your primary edge comes from the fact that you won't be drawing to less than the nuts. That is, after the flop, you should draw only to the nuts.

In games where people play approximately correctly, you must play not only correctly on the flop but also very tightly before the flop. Notice that there are two different strategies. In a really good game, the primary strategy is to play correctly and tightly on the flop. In a game that is not so good, you still have an edge as long as you play fewer hands before the flop than your opponents.

When playing low-limit Omaha eight-or-better, if you are simply the tightest player both before the flop and on the flop, you have a significant edge. However, if the game is fairly good, you will cost yourself a lot of profit if you play too tightly before the flop. For example, an ace-deuce in a loose game is almost always profitable, even if your other cards are nothing special. This is because if the flop gives you a low or a draw to a low, other players with ace-trey or deuce-trey will draw to the second and third nuts.

But if the game is reasonably tough, your ace-deuce loses most of its profitability, since other players won't be drawing to the second and third nuts as often. And when the low does come, you may have to split the low half, plus there will be fewer people to collect from. (Even so, an ace-deuce is usually still worth playing.)

185

Because Omaha eight-or-better has the same structure as Texas hold 'em, and because even reasonably good players tend to find reasons to play certain hands, if you just play tight before the flop, you will beat even the toughest games. (This should change as more people study this text.) But remember, in the looser games, you will cost yourself some profit.

There is a lot more play to this game than there appears to be. For example, if someone bets, you might need to raise to squeeze another player off a low draw when you also have a low draw. Even though it doesn't seem that you can knock out an ace-deuce draw, sometimes it doesn't pay for an opponent to draw after the flop. Consequently, if he plays well, he just might throw away his hand. (This works against only a few very good players.)

Even before the flop, you sometimes must make plays like reraising to knock out players behind you so that you are last to act. It is very advantageous to have the last position. It also is often good to be first to act. Problems can occur when you are in the middle.

The idea is to play hands that can develop into two-way hands, where you can either scoop or three-quarter an opponent. For example, suppose you have

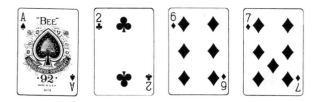

You may wish to raise, because you don't want someone holding a hand like

to also play in a multiway pot.

Notice that this player can make a higher straight than you can make, plus you can get quartered by tying for the low with some other player. Again, there is a lot more to this game than just playing technically correct.

The hands that tend to do well are those containing ace-deuce and ace-deuce-trey. Having a suited card with the ace is also beneficial. In a lot of spots, four high cards do well, because if this hand wins, there probably will not be a low.

Three big cards that include an ace, plus a deuce or a trey, are also good hands. But if the other low card with the ace is not a deuce or a trey, you should throw the hand away.

For example,

almost always should be discarded. This hand might become playable only if your opponents are playing very poorly and you can see the flop for one bet, or if you are in a very late position and no one has raised.

Also, note that when two low cards hit the board, all high hands go way down in value. Assuming that you win the high, you are now likely to split the pot if another low card comes.

More Specific Ideas

Following are a few specific concepts that will contribute to playing a winning Omaha eight-or-better game against competition that is *fairly weak*.

Concept No. 1: Don't play middle-sized cards. This includes hands like

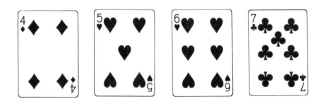

and

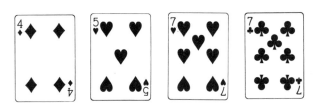

The problem with playing these kinds of hands is that you can't make the nuts, barring an occasional exception.

Concept No. 2: Middle straight cards are terrible. A hand like

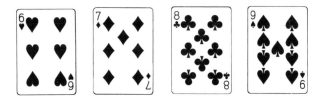

is quite a bit worse than a hand like

This is because if you make the nut straight with the first hand, the low is out there. Four high cards aren't terrific, but they usually are playable, especially if you also have a pair (which occasionally will enable you to make a big full house).

Concept No. 3: You don't have to play two aces. A pair of aces with nothing else going for it, such as two aces without even a flush draw, generally should be thrown away in early position. However, if there is no raising, you can call with a weak two-ace hand, hoping to hit your set.

Concept No. 4: Other hands to discard in *early position* are ace-trey and deuce-trey with nothing else. Ace-deuce is usually always worth playing, although with nothing else, your hand frequently should be discarded for a cold raise against tight players. In fact, a weak ace-deuce may not even be worth playing if a lot of tight players are in the game.

The weaker lows, when you have nothing else working, usually should be thrown away from early position, even if the game is fairly good. Keep in mind that Omaha eight-or-better is a highly positional game, and a weak ace-trey or deuce-trey usually will cost you money in early position. The exception is when the game has one or more extremely live players.

Concept No. 5: Four low cards without an ace can be a good starting hand. A hand like

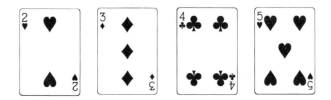

is not so bad, because if an ace hits, your lows are good. But you must have an ace for your low. So if the pot is multiway and no ace flops, be prepared to throw this hand away. However, it depends on exactly what comes out. If the flop is

you might want to play, since you can make a wheel, a six-high straight, or a full house. But if a lot of players took the flop, someone probably is drawing at a better low. That is, unless an ace hits, you most likely will be playing only for high and not for a very good high.

If the flop in the example given shows a two flush, you should throw away your hand unless you are getting high pot odds. But if no two flush is on board, it may be OK to continue playing.

Concept No. 6: In good position, ace-trey is almost always worth playing before the flop, but deuce-trey is usually not. There is a great deal of difference between an ace-trey and a deuce-trey. The ace-trey is significantly better, because it not only is lower than deuce-trey but also gives you more ways to win high, such as pairing aces. The deuce-trey is playable in very soft games, but you need an ace to flop.

Concept No. 7: High pairs with two other big cards are usually playable. In fact, in a multiway pot, a hand like

might be slightly better than a hand like

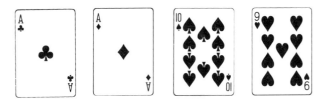

Also, in multiway pots, the aces you need are probably out in the low hands, which now makes the K♣K♦Q♠J♥ more of a live hand. With the kings, you have more straight draws to nut hands that won't split the pot, plus if you flop a set of kings, as opposed to a set of aces, you are more likely to win the whole pot. (The ace puts a low card on board.) This doesn't mean that you should play a pair of kings stronger than a pair of aces, because when you hold two kings, an ace can come to beat you.

With a hand like K♣K♦Q♠J♥, raising before the flop is usually not correct. Most of the preflop raising in this game is done strictly to knock out players behind you, that is, to buy the button. Raising before the flop to get more money in the pot is normally not the best strategy. Although with a hand like

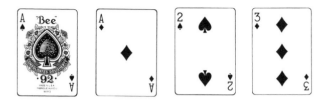

you generally will want to go ahead and raise.

Concept No. 8: Position means a lot. You can play more hands in the last couple of positions than in the early positions. This might be more true in tougher games, but it is also true in the loose, easy games that are common at the lower limits. (In late position, you have an opportunity to win additional money when you get a lucky flop.)

For example, in very late position, you can play a hand like

provided you can get in cheap. You also can play hands like

and

provided the conditions are right.

However, you still shouldn't play the medium-sized hands. Remember, if you have a ten-nine in your hand and the flop is

this is not nearly as good as if you have a jack-ten in your hand and the flop is

The second hand is much better, because it is more likely that you will win the whole pot if you make a straight.

Concept No. 9: A lot of raising before the flop adds marginally to your profits, but it adds tremendously to your fluctuations. This should be obvious, as many hands are not that dissimilar in value. However, you still should play almost the same number of hands before the flop, because it is unlikely that the raising indicates your opponents have superior hands to what you normally should play. That is, they usually are raising with hands worse than what you require to enter the pot. So you now should throw away the marginal hands that you sometimes would play in late position.

If the pots get big, you are forced to play slightly looser on the flop. For example, you might go for a back-door low with an ace-deuce if you have something else, such as a back-door nut flush draw.

If most of the hands have a lot of action early, by watching you will see exactly what the raising was done with, which will give you a good idea as to what you can play. These big pots may make it correct for you to take off another card. Since the game is Omaha, you often will pick up other possibilities and go to the end.

Concept No. 10: When you start jamming early, you add only a little bit to your edge, unless some terrible players are in the pot. There is a great deal of luck between your starting hand and the flop in Omaha eight-or-better, especially if other players in the pot might be playing a hand similar to what you hold.

Concept No. 11: Beware of trap hands on the flop. Suppose the flop is

If you have several opponents, you should throw away a trey-four with a jack-high flush draw. Although you have a low draw, a straight draw, and a flush draw, none is the nuts. Your hand should be discarded even if a lot of money is in the pot.

But played heads up, this hand is not so bad, except against someone who won't gamble. There are many times when you make the flush and it's good, or when you buy a jack and it is good. Your opponent easily could have something like

Even if the pots are multiway before the flop, they sometimes become heads up on the flop.

Concept No. 12: Stick to those hands that can make the nuts.
You can't profitably play a hand that does not have a draw to the nuts, unless you are heads up and the hand has many different possibilities.

There are some other exceptions. For example, you might call with middle or bottom trips if it looks like the right spot. Even hands like top two pair or just a pair of aces sometimes win the whole pot. But when many players are in, which is frequently the case at the lower limits, you usually will need the nuts or close to it to rake in any chips.

Concept No. 13: High hands lose value against low hands.
Once you know that you are going to be up against a made low hand, a high hand loses most of its value. For example, if the flop is

and you have a set of eights, your hand is not very good. Even though you currently have the nuts for high, any card except three of the sevens or the case eight can beat you. In addition, a low probably has already been made. Notice that a set of nines would be quite a bit better with an analogous flop like 9♠3♠2♥. (But you don't play a pair of nines in this game.)

Concept No. 14: Back-door potential or a lot of outs may make your hand playable. Drawing to hands that are not the nuts might be worth it if you have back-door potential or a lot of different outs. For example, suppose you hold

and the flop comes

giving you an ace-trey draw. Notice that you are drawing only to a deuce for the nut low. But a king may win the whole pot for you, and another spade gives you the nut flush draw. If there is not a lot of action, this hand is worth taking a card off.

If you make an ace-trey low, you have to decide whether you should pay off a bet. That is, you must play poker well. If you are caught in a jam, throw away your hand. But if it is a bet and a call, you definitely should also call. Remember, the pot easily can contain as many as a dozen bets, and both of your opponents may have high hands.

Concept No. 15: On the flop, when you are going low, don't "go to war" with very many hands. The exceptions are when you can't get counterfeited, you have an ace-high flush draw, or you have other back-door straight or nut flush potential. An example of the first condition is when you have a hand like

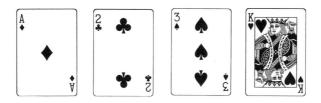

and the flop comes

Notice that being unable to get counterfeited is a much stronger reason for challenging your opponent than either of the other two conditions.

Concept No. 16: You sometimes can "go to war" early with just top set. You don't mind going to war when you have top set, there is no low draw, and you are against a maniac type player who easily could have a smaller set. For example, suppose you hold two kings and the flop comes

Against certain types of opponents, a raising war — even early in the hand — might be correct. However, if three or more opponents are in the pot and you think you may be against a big

wrap-around straight draw, it might be best to slow down and see how things develop. (There is more discussion of this topic later in the text.)

Concept No. 17: When you have made your low and are sure that you are getting quartered, you may have to throw away your hand. Suppose you have an ace-deuce in your hand and the flop comes

You are last to act, and five opponents ahead of you are betting, raising, and reraising. In this situation, you probably should discard your hand. Notice that you have no high and obviously will be splitting the low with at least one other player.

Concept No. 18: When you play an ace-trey in a multiway pot and flop a low draw, it is often correct to throw away your hand. This is one of those spots where you must play poker well. But if you have nothing else to go with your low draw, you probably should fold. If you have some other good possibilities, be more inclined to play. For example, there might be a dozen cards that could turn to give you a straight draw for the nuts. If this is the case, consider taking another card off. Otherwise, it is best to fold.

Concept No. 19: There are some bluffing opportunities. Here's an example. Suppose the flop comes

and there is a bet. You sometimes can raise with virtually nothing. In a short-handed pot, your opponent might have bet an ace-ten figuring that you hold low cards. If you have a hand like

a raise is not unreasonable. Notice that your hand has a lot of ways to turn into a winner or a split. Also notice that this type of play works best in short-handed pots. In pots with many players, it is best to never attempt such a bluff.

Concept No. 20: You don't have to push an ace-deuce. Suppose on fourth street that you have an ace-deuce and nothing else, but you have the low hand made. The action goes bet, call, call, and now it is your turn. You usually should just call in this situation, because a reraise by the original bettor can knock out the other callers.

However, whether to raise also depends on your judgment of the original bettor. For example, if he is a tight player who almost always goes for low, he probably has an ace-deuce. If you have made a medium pair to go along with your low, his reraise could knock out everyone else, and you may win the high. Always remember to consider the play of the hand. Another problem is that the last card might be an ace or a deuce to counterfeit you.

Concept No. 21: On the end, it is sometimes incorrect to raise even when you have the nuts. Here's an example. Suppose that you are last to act in a four-person pot and the board is

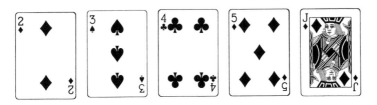

If all you have is a wheel, you are probably against one or perhaps two other wheels, as well as a flush. You may want to check if it is checked to you. And if there is a lot of action before it gets to you, depending on the pot odds, you might want to fold.

Concept No. 22: On the end, you should raise with an ace-deuce in a four-handed pot but not in a three-handed pot. If someone else also has an ace-deuce, you lose money by raising in a three-handed pot. In a four-handed pot, you will break even. The exceptions to not raising in a three-handed pot are if you play well and are fairly sure that you are not against another ace-deuce, or if you are against an opponent who is extremely live.

Basic Strategy

Afterthought

Keep in mind that there is more to playing Omaha eight-or-better than just drawing to the nuts. Of course, if a lot of people are calling all the way — which is often the case at the smaller limits — then just playing for cinches is all you need to do to win a small amount. But if you have a fairly good understanding of the game in general and the current situation in particular, you should be able to do much better.

When playing, you will notice that some players generally will raise or reraise when they think they have a good hand. Needless to say, these are not people who have a good understanding of the game, although most of them will believe they play very well. This is an example of how Omaha eight-or-better can fool people. Consequently, if you have a good grasp of everything covered so far, you should be able to hold your own in most games played in a public cardroom.

Part Two

Advanced Strategy

Advanced Strategy

Introduction

In the major cardrooms that offer Omaha eight-or-better, there usually will be a small number of games (perhaps only one) at $10-$20 and lower, and there might be a big game with a much higher limit. Frequently sitting at the big game will be several well-known and highly skilled players. Most of the other players in the game also will play well.

Omaha eight-or-better at the higher limits is generally a much different game from what I have discussed so far. Many of the pots will be contested short-handed. Players won't automatically go to the end if they have a draw to second or third nuts. There even will be some opportunities to bluff. Also, hands that you can "accidentally" back into often will become important.

Just playing for cinches, even though making one is nice, won't get the job done. Omaha eight-or-better at the higher limits becomes a real poker game. You now will have to play poker well.

General Concepts

In this section of the text, I am referring to advanced players and medium- to high-stakes games. Common limits are $50-$100 and $75-$150. Many of the players are highly skilled, and to expect to have good results, you need to play very well. If you just draw to cinches, don't expect to do much better than break even.

Basically, this is a game of trying to get in cheaply before the flop. If you are putting in a lot of money early, it is usually not so much to get in money with a quality hand, but to knock out players so you have a positional advantage. This allows you to use your poker skills later and to play against the blinds or perhaps the blinds and a weaker hand.

The big decision is to analyze the flop and understand how it relates to your hand and whether you should play on. Playing on or folding (once the flop comes) is not always as automatic as some people think.

Most people tend to play too loose after the flop, so you get an opportunity to flop hands and play with people who are taking the worst of it. Generally, when a lot of players take the flop, you must have the nut low draw, the nut low made *with redraws*, or a very strong high hand to continue.

In this game, most of the money you make is not from your skillful play; it is usually from your opponents' poor play. They often call and try to win the pot with a second- or third-best hand, without playing forcefully and perhaps knocking out someone else.

There is also a lot to think about in Omaha eight-or-better. In general, however, the decisions are slightly more obvious in this game than in some other forms of poker. When you start your hand, it is usually clear-cut how to play and which is the best path to take when you play a hand out.

One of the big skill factors is understanding how the other players play their hands and playing your hand accordingly. This makes Omaha eight-or-better a lot different from most other forms of poker, where even though you play your hand based on how your opponents play, you don't alter your betting as much. As an example, it might be right to check and fold the nuts in Omaha eight-or-better, something that would be totally unheard of in a game like Texas hold 'em.

In Omaha eight-or-better, how your opponent plays can determine whether you will even enter the pot. For instance, a profitable hand against timid opponents can be a trash hand against the same number of players if they are aggressive. Thus accurately gauging your opponents is a skill that all advanced players need to develop.

The secret of this game is to have the nuts with draws to better hands. It is vital to add up the chances of back-door flushes, back-door straights, and miracle cards, plus the draws that you don't expect can come to defeat you. Your chances of winning can be reduced by as much as 10 percent — or far greater in some extreme cases — when you have the best hand but with no chance to redraw. For example, suppose you figure that your hand has 50 percent value, assuming that there are no redraws against you. In reality, your hand may have only 40 percent value because of the redraws. (Notice that when I say 10 percent, I mean 10 percent of 100, not 10 percent of your hand value.)

The 10 percent is just a rough figure based on experience. But the point is that in multiway pots, your hand is almost never as strong as it appears to be (even when it is the nuts), because these redraws are almost always there. Consequently, it is important to have all four cards working well together so you have back-door possibilities. This may allow you to take some pots back or, at times, to three-quarter your opponent instead of splitting the pot.

Position

Position is critical. You probably want to play very few hands up front due to the large amount of jamming that occurs. If first to act, you will be forced to fold in many good situations. Even though you have check-and-raise available, you will not be able to use it, because in many cases when the action gets back to you, the pot will have been raised and reraised already.

Being last to act is a big advantage. Consequently, very few hands, other than the absolute premium ones, should be played in early position.

If the game is tight, which is usually the case in only some of the high-stakes games, you will want to play few hands up front and to steal a lot of pots in the back. If the game is very loose, stealing becomes unimportant, as you virtually never have the opportunity to try it.

When you attempt to steal from a late position before the flop, you usually get action. But you still want to play a lot of weaker hands from this spot. You should bring them in with a raise, because many players — even when they are in late position — won't play without ace-deuce, ace-trey, or some other big hand. So your raise will tend to run these players out, and you often will end up playing against the blinds, who will take a flop with a weak hand to see what is out there. Thus, you not only will have position on the blinds, but also will frequently have the better hand. Notice that this is a very good situation when playing short-handed, especially if you are heads up.

Low Hands

Assuming that the game you are in is very loose, you will want to play any four cards, suited up if possible, that include an ace-deuce or an ace-trey. The exception is when many players already have entered the pot. In this case, you often will get quartered with these hands, unless you are against very bad players. In multiway pots, you will want to have a third low card, such as an ace-deuce-trey or an ace-deuce-four, or four low cards with the ace in your hand. A lot of the low hands will get counterfeited by one of your low cards coming out on fourth or fifth street. You will be putting your money in with a cinch, yet if one of the cards that counterfeits your hand appears on a later street, you will get nothing from the pot. In other words, having a third low card, even if it is not that good, is very important in big multiway confrontations. Since many players will be going for low hands, you need that additional out.

With tremendous low hands, such as three or four low cards that also might be suited up, you don't mind putting in more money early, because much of the time you will flop a playable hand. Also, if a lot of money goes in early, you probably will still take a card off to see fourth street. One reason that you go to fourth street when the flop is not very favorable is that if higher cards come early, there rarely will be more than one high hand with strength. Thus the pot won't get jammed.

On the other hand, if low cards come, the high hand is the one that gets jammed in. This is because there are usually a couple of players drawing at the cinch low with possible straight or flush draws to go with it. Although it is not always the case, a general rule is: *Jammed pots when low cards flop usually mean several low draws.*

Ace-deuce is not automatically a giant hand and the kind of hand to wait for. It plays better in a low-stakes game, where there are almost always players who consistently draw at the third and fourth (or even worse) low hands. However, as the game progresses in stakes, players seldom draw at non-nut low hands, unless they have a high hand working with it or unless there is a "live one" in the pot.

High Hands

High hands do well in situations where no low card or only one comes on the flop. When two or three low cards come on the flop, high hands tend to do poorly.

High hands also do well in games where the pot is not raised before the flop, since it is more likely than not that two or more low cards to an eight will come out on the flop. Most of the flops are going to be unplayable unless you hit a really big hand. Two high cards and two low cards make it tough to hit a big high hand, unless it is the nut flush draw or possibly top set. However, top set often can be trouble, because low straights and flushes are fairly easy to make. Consequently, you want to play more high hands in games where it does not cost much to see the flop.

Remember, when you are playing the high cards, you need to get in cheap early if the action is multiway. If the action is not multiway, it doesn't matter, because high hands play well short-handed. Many players will disagree with this, but in a tight game with only one or two players calling against you, double-suited high hands do very well since three low cards don't always appear. When they do appear, they may not make your opponents' hands. For example, suppose the flop comes

and you have

210

giving you a set. You are against an opponent who holds

If either an ace or a deuce appears on a later street and no other low card comes, your high hand will scoop the pot. However, when you are against many opponents, someone will make a low.

What you want to avoid in this game is playing when it looks as though other people might be counterfeiting your hand. For instance, a hand like

is usually a good hand. But it's not so good if a couple of other players also are playing high with similar big cards, since your hand is probably somewhat counterfeited by their hands. When you flop a straight or a big wrap-around draw, they may flop high trips, which will take much value away from your hand.

You want to play the high hands in short-handed pots — preferably heads up — against players who play only the low hands. High hands don't do well against players who play extremely tight and are likely to have a hand like two aces with low cards. In this case, you become a big percentage dog to win the pot. Moreover, it is easy to get outplayed, and you often will have to throw away your hand since your opponents have hands that can go a lot further.

Having a hand that can go further without much early improvement is an advantage in split games, because this hand has more opportunity for overall improvement. Also, your opponent can bet for value more often or bluff and knock you out early when you would have had a winning hand at a later stage.

In heads-up situations, the high hand is usually the favorite over four low cards without an ace. However, the four low cards often will be able to outplay the high hand, since the flops will tend to get scary and the high hand will have to go out.

When playing the high hands heads up, you have to call a lot of times and see how the hand develops. You often will split the pot with a low hand, but sometimes you will scoop the whole pot. However, when the board becomes real scary and a player shows strength, you will have to get out.

Assuming that you are an advanced player, you should be able to read your opponent and have a good indication of how strong he is and to determine whether you have a split or a probable loser. If you think your hand is a likely loser, you frequently should fold. Making these decisions well is where some real skill comes in the game. With work, you eventually can develop the requisite skill to correctly assess these situations, and this will add significantly to your winning percentage.

Here are a few hints that will help you in this area.

1. Pay attention to the game. This includes observing not only those hands you play, but all other hands as well.

2. Try to understand the meaning of someone's check, bet, or raise. Does your opponent bet or raise only when he has the nuts? Is he willing to make a play, especially short-handed?

3.   Is anyone currently steaming? If someone has just absorbed a couple of "beats" and you think this has affected him, you may want to call him down with a marginal hand.

4.   When in a tough situation, take all the time you need to make your decision. This may include reconstructing the hand in your mind from the beginning and trying to determine the best course of action.

5.   Spend time away from the table thinking about some of your tougher hands. This may be the most helpful hint of all.

You don't want to play high hands too aggressively when the flop is such that a lot of scare cards can come to beat you. This is particularly true when you flop a set and the other two cards on board are close together. For example, suppose you have

and the flop comes

Even though you have a set of jacks, an ace or a king can give someone else a larger set. An ace, a deuce, a five, a six, or a seven can make a low straight. Any spade can make someone a flush. An ace, deuce, five, six, seven, or eight can put the low out, and an eight, nine, ten, queen, king, or ace also can give someone a straight draw to beat you. Notice that you won't really know whether to continue playing or to fold after fourth street.

This type of situation may not be avoidable. Consequently, when you are in a multiway pot and find yourself in one of these spots, you should play very cautiously. The scare cards often will come, and you will run the risk of being jammed in when you don't have the best hand.

It is difficult to scoop a big pot with just the high hand, because big pots usually don't develop unless someone has the low locked up. If the pot is multiway and no one has a low hand made, don't expect the pot to be jammed (even though there are quite a few hands that would be worth jamming if you knew that someone else had the current lock high and you had a draw at a low with some other draws).

An exception is when two players have the same high hand with the lows tagging along. If one of the high hands also has a redraw and hits it, he can win a monster pot. However, these types of hands are infrequent.

In conclusion, the high hands do very well in heads-up pots and short-handed pots. In the big multiway pots, when three low cards are on board, or in the jammed-up pots, the high hands will either win half the pot or get scooped. Consequently, as you see the pot developing, you can start speculating on the value of your hand and make appropriate strategy decisions. You may decide that the best way to play your high hand is simply to throw it away.

Your Starting Hand

Since you don't know what four cards your opponent holds, you always can speculate on how this hand will do against that hand and which is a better starting hand. However, except for the absolute best starting hands, any hand you have can be counterfeited by a similar starting hand either one notch higher or slightly lower with an additional draw.

Although your hand won't be counterfeited every time, it happens a lot in multiway pots. This is why you must be careful with many hands that look reasonably good. But in short-handed pots, you have to play these hands out and play good poker. (Playing good poker includes understanding how your opponent plays, how the board cards relate not only to your hand but also to the type of cards that your opponent plays, and how your opponent perceives you at that given moment.)

Most hands run very close, usually less than a 3-to-2 favorite heads up. Consequently, the most important skill is the ability to outplay your opponent.

Low hands tend to have a playing advantage over high hands, because scare cards often appear and the holder of the high hand does not know what to do. However, the low hands also have some disadvantages, which usually occur when the high hand is forcing them to call all the bets. Thus there is a tradeoff on both sides. As previously mentioned, the high hands do well heads up. But in multiway pots, they must make very big hands and frequently need redraws to ensure their profitability.

For example, if a third low card comes on the river, besides making a low hand, it also might give someone a small straight that can beat a high set. But if this card also gives the high hand a flush, enabling the high hand to lock up the high side, then it is not so bad. These redraws are extremely important, as straights frequently come out and you need the redraws (which also can give you the low) so you don't get scooped as often.

An ace is a key card in this game, because it is needed to make the nut low when there is no ace on the board. Also, it makes the nut flush when it is suited up. These draws come through a lot, and some of them are back-door plays. Finally, when the ace makes a straight on the high side, it is of course the nut straight.

You want to play hands that include an ace, although you must realize that in a multiway pot, one or more of your opponents also probably holds an ace. In this case, it is less likely that another ace will come out for low. It is also important that your ace be suited with some other card in your hand, because when a lot of people are in, it is likely that you will be against someone who holds an ace-deuce or an ace-trey.

In general, there are few starting hands that you should play where all four cards are not closely interweaved. Unless you hold an ace-deuce, which does not always require all four cards working together, consistently starting with three or fewer coordinated cards will prove to be very costly. You sometimes can play just a dry ace-deuce, particularly if there are live players in your game who regularly play any two low cards. Another possible exception to playing only coordinated cards might be a hand like ace-trey-four-ten, with the ace suited to one of the other cards. But even this hand has some of the cards working well together, though not necessarily all four of them.

The reason it is so important to have all four cards working together is that many pots get jammed on the later streets, and you often will need the extra outs — that is, draws or redraws to better hands that these cards provide. As stated earlier, these extra outs are the secret of this game.

A lot of other hands may be tempting, but you are dealt enough of the totally coordinated hands that you don't need to fool around with weaker hands, unless the pot will be played heads up, which makes a major difference. This idea is important in other forms of Omaha, but it is even more important in Omaha eight-or-better, because you tend to get jammed so much on the later streets.

Starting With Big Pairs

Two aces is a key hand in Omaha eight-or-better. With a deuce — and to a lesser extent a trey — included, you can consider two aces a premium hand. The bad part of having a pair of bullets is that when you make three of a kind with the aces, one of the cards needed to make a low hand that can cost you half the pot is now on board. However, an ace on board won't make that many straights. If you make, let's say, three fours with two fours in your hand, the threat of running into a straight (not to mention a bigger set) is now greater.

On the other hand, if you make a high set, such as three kings, you have eliminated one possible low card on board, which means that it is not as likely that someone will share a low with you. As stated earlier, this is a major advantage of holding a pair of kings.

However, when you make three aces and also have a low draw, you have a chance to win both sides in a multiway pot. But if you flop three kings, the pot is not likely to be multiway unless two low cards are also on board, in which case your hand is severely diminished.

When you have two aces without a good low card, you can't stand a lot of action before the flop unless you are suited up or have four high cards. For example, suppose you hold

This hand should be thrown away if there is any kind of action early, because neither ace is suited with either of the other two cards. Also notice that if there is any kind of strong action, it is

likely that someone else has an ace and he probably holds ace-deuce. Thus the chances of your making three aces or better have diminished. This means that you are not playing on the strength of your aces anymore but need to rely on your other combinations, so they have to be extra strong.

This makes two aces a peculiar hand. In fact, if there is a lot of action, the aggressive raiser may hold the other two aces, which really cripples your hand.

Other big pairs do poorly unless the pot is short-handed, the flop comes with three high cards (in which case no low can come out), or the pairs are joined by two other related high cards.

As the big cards get lower, their value drops way off. This is because when you make straights, it puts low cards on board, which of course will give your opponents opportunities to make lows. For example, any hand you hold that includes an eight-nine or a nine-ten will split the pot almost automatically if you make a straight with a five-six-seven or a six-seven-eight on board. So the potential of being able to scoop the pot with a high hand is greatly reduced. In fact, a hand like

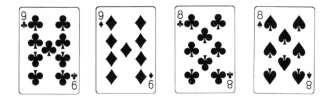

is close to the worst four cards that you can be dealt. Those of you who consistently play these types of hands will have no chance in this game.

When You Are First In

The difference between tight and loose games as to whether you should bring it in with a raise or a call is extremely important. A call will tend to promote multiway pots, but you usually should raise if you are hoping to narrow the field to three or fewer players.

If the game is loose, you can expect multiway pots whether you just call or bring it in with a raise. In this situation, you should play according to what best fits your style. But if the game is loose and there is a lot of raising, you may want to just call to see who does the raising so you can gauge the strengths of the various hands.

If it is a loose game where players tend to call and not raise much, then with your better hands, you may want to bring it in with a raise. This is because you will not gain much information when your opponents just call.

If you are playing in a tight game, you probably will bring it in for a raise most of the time, hoping to steal the blinds (and being happy to do so) or to play against only the blinds, who often will be weak. Your raise frequently will drive out the players behind you. Thus you most likely will be playing against the blinds, who will be out of position. If you don't bring it in with a raise, you are likely to find yourself caught in the middle, since there usually will be callers behind you (even though the game is tight), as well as the blinds. This puts you in a tough situation. However, if you are playing well, you are likely to have the best hand or the best draw(s), which should compensate some for your poor position.

In general, you should not raise a lot unless the game is tight and you are confident that you can get in a heads-up confrontation. When heads up, you should be able to outplay many of your weaker opponents.

Also, when playing heads up, you can win the high with very weak hands (such as a pair of tens), plus you can bluff players out since most of your opponents will play for low. That is, if high cards come, a lot of players will be quick to fold their hands. Some of your opponents automatically will throw away top pair and even two pair if they are heads up. So when you flop two pair or top pair with an ace kicker, your bet sometimes will make your opponent fold, even when his hand is as good as yours or slightly better.

How To Play Your Hand

When you first look at your hand and make the decision to play it, you must determine exactly how you want to play. Specifically, do you want lots of opponents or a few opponents? A big pot or a small pot? This depends on the type of players who are behind you, your position, and the game itself. Even how you are doing in the game might have some bearing. This is not usually the case, but if you have limited chips and want to play longer, you probably should play hands where you keep the pot small early and put more money in later with your better hands. Notice that this will keep your fluctuations down. On the other hand, you might have a slightly larger expectation by putting in more money early with some of your better hands, but this approach also may increase your fluctuations as much as threefold.

The decision whether to jam the pot and get all the raises in or to keep the pot smaller will be based mainly on the strength of your hand. For instance, if you are raising and reraising, you usually should have the nuts, especially if you are on the low side. However, you also should consider how easy it is for your hand to be counterfeited later on, or how easy it is for a scare card to come that may prevent your opponent (the one going for the other side, who is currently your ally) from jamming on a later street.

If it is easy for your hand to get counterfeited, you may not want to give a lot of action until all the cards are out. But suppose you have the high and you want the player with the probable low to jam it. He might fear that if a small card comes on a later street, his hand can be ruined, or perhaps he may just be afraid to bet. This may prevent the action you are hoping for later in the hand. If you think this can happen, you might want to jam it early.

Notice that these decisions are more subtle than most. This is where experience and thinking about the game will prove to be very helpful; advanced players excel because they play poker well and think along the right lines.

A little deception early can go a long way, because many players will form an opinion about your cards and stick with it all the way through the hand. Consequently, on an early round, you occasionally should not raise in a spot where most other players will raise, and sometimes you should bet with a marginal hand when most of your opponents won't. These types of plays can be beneficial later in the hand when the jamming starts. Someone might misread your hand and give you lots of action with the second-best hand when you hold the best hand.

Play on the Flop

Any time that an ace hits on the flop, you have to tighten up significantly. As noted previously, an ace is a key card that can go either high or low. Many high hands can get counterfeited by people making three aces and aces full, and an ace also can make a lot of the low hands, especially against those players who wait for premium low hands like ace-deuce-trey.

Notice that if an ace hits the board with another low card, an opponent can now have the nut low draw with a pair of aces and possibly other draws working. Not only does this devalue your high hand, but you also may be against a two-way hand that might not need further improvement, except in a big multiway pot where a lot of strong hands will be made. When an ace flops and is one of two suited cards, it is less probable that someone may make the nut flush, because the better players are reluctant to play a king with a suited card. But when a two flush that does not include an ace comes on the flop, it is more likely that a nut flush draw is out, since an ace with a suited card is a hand that most people like to play.

Suppose the flop comes

and you hold two queens. In a multiway pot, this type of flop easily could give someone else a wrap-around straight draw, which means that any card between a nine and an ace might complete the straight. If there is a fair amount of money in the pot already, it is correct for you (the player with the big set) to raise or perhaps to try for a check-raise in an effort to knock out other players who have (so far) only three cards to a low, even though the possible straight draw puts you at risk. If players with a low draw aren't forced out and low cards come, one of your opponents may back into a straight that can beat your three queens.

Now suppose you are in a multiway pot and have a wrap-around straight draw with the flop given in the example. You would not want to knock out other players, because you must complete your straight to win the pot and most of the cards that will make your hand will not bring the lows into play. Thus, even though you have a high hand, you want all the lows in, while someone with a big set would want them out.

Of course, if you have a wrap-around straight draw and think one of your opponents has a similar hand, you probably would want to eliminate all players with low draws. By doing so, you might end up splitting for high with no one getting a low (you won't get quartered), you may scoop the pot with just a high pair, or if low cards come, you might be able to bluff your opponent out.

As can be seen from this discussion, in Omaha eight-or-better, there are frequently different ways to play your hand. You should spend some time both at and away from the table thinking about some of these situations, since the immediate obvious strategy may not always be the best approach.

When You
Have the Best Hand

When you have what you believe to be the best hand, you usually will either bet or raise, except possibly on the flop. You sometimes should wait for fourth street to see whether a scare card or a counterfeit card comes to knock you off. For example, suppose you hold

and the flop comes

If the pot is multiway, it is likely for there to be nut straights out for the high, as well as other lows, meaning that this could be a jammed hand. Since all you have is a low, you want to be extremely careful before you put much money in or start the jamming, even though you currently have a cinch for low. It is easy for an ace or a deuce to come, which will now counterfeit your hand, causing you to lose everything. If it is already jammed, a fold is in order. You are playing for a quarter (or perhaps less) of the pot, and your cinch low may cost you money even if it does not get counterfeited.

This is certainly a time to slow down the action and then gamble later in the hand. With this type of flop, you are going to get action since people will play anyway. Consequently, there is no sense in putting a lot of money in on the flop when you may need to throw away your hand later. Investing too much too soon is a mistake that many intermediate players make.

This brings up a related point. When cautious players do not have redraws, they almost never raise with an ace-deuce until all the cards are out. If you are playing against a tight player, there is a possible nut low out, and he is in there calling, he usually has it. You often can put this type of player on the cinch with no redraws and no draws at the high. If you are against him in a short-handed pot and an ace or a deuce hits, which counterfeits your hand, you may be able to bluff him out since his hand also will be ruined.

This conservative approach makes money at the smaller limits and in the loose games at the higher stakes. But in tight games, it doesn't work, because good players just won't give the tight players action. When the experts are in the pot with cautious tight players, the experts usually have them quartered or will check it along with them so the pots stay small, and they won't pay off on the end.

Advanced Strategy

Afterthought

As you have seen, the secret to Omaha eight-or-better is to make the nuts with redraws. Of course, these hands don't occur very often, which is why you must have a good understanding of the opponent you are up against.

Likewise, position is critical. You can steal a lot if the games are tight. There also are opportunities to bluff, which usually occur when high cards flop in short-handed pots.

Keep in mind that the low hands can stand more action than the high hands. And in a multiway pot, just having a dry ace-deuce is not good enough. But most important, make sure that you are protected against being counterfeited. It is vital to have all four of your cards working together, whether you hold a high hand or a low hand.

In addition, you need to determine whether you want the pot to be large or small, and whether the time is right to start jamming. Knowing exactly how you want to play your hand — before the flop, on the flop, and after the flop — is crucial in this game. Should you bet or raise, or should you check and wait to make sure that your hand does not get counterfeited? These are decisions you must constantly make.

Part Three

Additional Advanced Concepts

Additional Advanced Concepts

Introduction

In the preceding section, I covered many of the important factors that are required to produce a winning strategy in Omaha eight-or-better. But as in most forms of poker, there is always more to optimal winning play.

The previous material is — of course — absolutely essential, but to become an expert, you need a complete grasp of the game and all its nuances. This includes comprehending concepts that do not fall under the heading of strategy, such as fluctuations. Understanding the natural swings of the game will help you to always play your best — that is, it will cut down on your steaming.

In addition, understanding how your playing style interacts with that of your opponent — which might be different from his normal playing style if he is emotionally out of control — is very important. You must know how to play in loose games, in tight games, and against very tight opponents, as well as the proper strategy adjustments for heads-up play, three-handed play, and play in multiway pots. Many of these ideas are difficult to master, and failing to understand them is the downfall of many players. But with experience and the proper knowledge (which, of course, includes reading this book and thinking about the game), you can become proficient in these areas.

Automatic Play

The play of many hands frequently becomes automatic. For example, in a heads-up pot, suppose you flop two pair and it looks as though your opponent has a low draw. You bet and a low card comes on the turn, so you now check and call through the river. In these situations, you often look at trips or straights, or your opponents show you lows, and you split or even win the whole pot.

As stated, a lot of these hands "come automatic." But you generally still have to play them out as just described, even though you don't know where you stand. You can't simply fold in these spots, because the pot frequently has already become fairly large.

Again, you should not play hands that can't go far. Conversely, if you flop what looks like the best hand, especially heads up, you have to punish your opponent.

Normally your opponent will play back when he has you beat. There is very little slow-playing in Omaha eight-or-better, so you should know about where you stand. Many players are afraid of a miracle card that can beat them, so they tend to play more straightforward. But if the pot is contested by a lot of players, some of your opponents will slow-play a bit more.

High Versus Low
in Three-Handed Pots

Suppose you are in a three-handed pot and there are one or two cards to come. You have a high hand that is not going to be easily beat, and it appears that both of your opponents have made good low hands or have good low draws that are either the nuts or close to the nuts. In this situation, you should not raise if one of the low hands bets, you are next, and the third player still remains to act behind you. By not raising, your half of the pot will be a little larger. Notice that you are in a situation where you are going to split the pot, and by just calling, you will be able to chop up the player behind you. If you raise, he probably will go out if he does not have the nuts or a draw to the nuts, and he may even fold a cinch if he realizes that he will be quartered.

However, if you think neither of your opponents will fold, you should start jamming.

On the other hand, if your high is weak and there is some chance that you can be beat, then it may be correct to try to drive out the third player. But if he has draws to a quality high to go along with his low, you might not succeed in getting the pot heads up.

On the river in a three-way pot, suppose a player who obviously has a high hand bets out first, the second player who appears to have a low just calls, and you have made the nut low. Automatically raising with your nut low is not correct. You have to consider how the person in the middle plays. If he is a weak player who would raise with the nut low but just call with a different low, then you can go ahead and jam the pot with the high player. But if the person in the middle is a fairly good player, then you probably should just call with the nut low, because he will be aware that you may have made the nut low with him and will be afraid that he (and you) will be quartered.

In addition, if the person in the middle figures that you are a decent player, he might not want to raise with the nut low, since he may think you can throw away a weaker low. Consequently, automatically raising in this spot with a cinch is wrong, as it is easy for you to be quartered. However, to not raise, you have to think there is more than a two-thirds chance you will be quartered, since a raise will win an extra half-bet when it works but will cost only a quarter of a bet (in a three-way pot) when it backfires.

Loose Games

Most games are considered loose when a lot of people are calling and raising. If the game is like this, you need hands that can make the nuts with draws and redraws to even better hands. An ace-deuce with no other draws will split the low or get counterfeited too often, in which case you lose everything. So you want hands that have the best low, or the best low draw with chances to back-door flushes, regular nut flush draws, straight draws, or trips, or a wheel with a chance of a six- or seven-high straight.

In big multiway pots, when you are holding one of these hands, you frequently will be able to make the low, which often will split with someone else, but sometimes to "hog" the high (or perhaps split the high). However, when there are many players and a lot of jamming, the nuts are usually out on both sides.

It's very important to have all four cards working together, as best as possible, and for those cards to be extra strong — that is, ace-deuce with two other good cards, ace-deuce-trey, or two aces with one or two low cards. Also, being suited adds a lot of value to your hand in a loose game. For example, on the flop, you might make a low and jam with it if you also have back-door or regular flush potential. If you now get lucky and complete the flush, you might scoop the pot or perhaps get three-quarters of it.

Bigger hands, such as four high straight cards suited up, don't do well in this type of game, unless the pot gets played short-handed or you can enter the pot cheaply. In these slightly looser games, which are typical at the smaller stakes tables with many people taking the flop, the high hands generally don't perform well.

An ace is a key card in loose games, and a suited ace adds much value to your hand. An ace suited with one of three low cards, such as

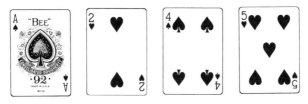

is a premium hand. Other premium hands include

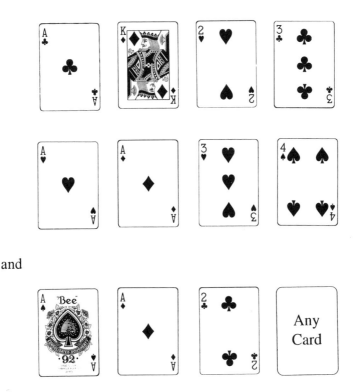

and

Remember, having a suited ace working, as you would in some of the hands illustrated, makes those hands even stronger.

Even four small cards can do very well, but they almost always require an ace to hit on the flop. You usually want to get in cheap with this holding and to have opponents who will gamble with you even if an ace comes. If an ace does not appear, be prepared to fold. (The odds are 3.3-to-1 against one or more aces appearing on the flop if you do not hold an ace in your hand.)

Multiway Versus Short-Handed Play

In multiway pots, you need very good hands. In short-handed pots, it doesn't matter as much. Of course, good hands always do better than poor hands, but most important in short-handed pots are position and playing against weaker opponents over whom you have good control.

For instance, suppose you have the best position and are heads up against a weak opponent whom you can maneuver well. All but your really trash hands have a good expectation, and you generally should play aggressively in this situation. If your opponent can't make a low, he usually folds, and unless he has a great high hand, he gets scared by any card that comes out.

Because typical players are accustomed to seeing so many cinches in multiway pots, they don't realize that in heads-up pots, they are not running into monster hands all the time. Consequently, many players are so "gun-shy" from seeing all the big hands that you can bluff and maneuver people when the pot is short-handed.

In a multiway pot, everyone is drawing at something, and many players usually are drawing at nut hands. They tend to stay in, and much of the time they have close to the proper equity to continue. Thus the outcome is usually determined by who catches the best hand. If you are capable of recognizing when this occurs, you will be able to get out at the proper time and will not get caught in a jam and lose a bunch of extra bets.

In Omaha eight-or-better, most people play scared because they frequently are up against the nuts. Because of this fear, especially in multiway pots, when someone comes out betting in an early position, he usually has the nuts or something close to it. It is unlikely that anyone other than a very good player will bet on the come or with a weak hand to see where he stands. So if players are playing as just described — that is, they are announcing the strength of their hands — you usually should get out unless you also have a big hand.

Announcing the strength of a hand does not cost very much in multiway pots, since enough players will tag along trying to draw out. So it doesn't necessarily hurt the player who announces his hand as much as it helps you to know not to get involved at that point.

If four or five players are in the pot, it is clear that they have fairly good hands, and you have a wrap-around hand with draws at both a good low and a good high — that is, you have lots of outs for both ways but these outs are not for the nuts — you still may have to fold. These kinds of hands, which are very strong in a heads-up situation, can easily be beat in a multiway pot, no matter which side you happen to hit. Thus, in pots with many players, these hands clearly can be folded, but in a heads-up pot, you can go ahead and raise or reraise with them.

Here's an example. Suppose you start with

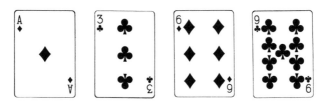

and the flop comes

Notice that a deuce, four, six, or eight will give you a low, but only the deuce will be the nuts. Also notice that a four or an eight will give you a straight, but only the eight will produce the nut straight. In addition, if a club gets there, someone else could make a higher flush. Hence, even though it appears that you have a lot of outs for both a high hand and a low hand, if many players are still in and it looks as though there may be a lot of action, you should fold. This is partly because those few times when you make the nuts, you have a high probability of being quartered, and most of the hands you make will just be flat-out losers.

However, if you are heads up and have a fairly big hand, you should play it as such. That is, go ahead and bet or raise, except if you are against a very tight player who almost has to have an ace-deuce, in which case most of your lows will get beat.

In a two-player pot, weak hands can be played in good position, and different two-way hands have a lot of value. But in a multiway pot, these hands are total trash. Hands that do very well in a multiway pot tend not to do as well in a heads-up pot.

For example, a hand like

does OK heads up. But because of its redraw possibilities, this hand is a very good holding if you expect many players.

In a three-handed pot, you are laying 2-to-1 on your side if you have only one side. This is one of the trickiest spots to be in, because frequently the pot becomes three-handed and you find yourself fighting for one of the halves. In this case, you may be taking the worst of it.

As you can see, the high hand in a short-handed pot tends to do better, because a low hand generally requires a lot of improvement to counterfeit the high hand. Also, you usually can tell when you are not competing against another high hand, unless you are against a low hand with some sort of high draw.

In a heads-up pot, the high hand is usually the best hand to have, but you also would like a low draw, even if it is a poor one. You may be sharing the high hand with your opponent, which happens more often than you might think, so having the chance to make a low on the river may get you three-quarters of the pot.

This situation can be reversed if your opponent has a better low draw than you do. Thus, even though you have the nuts heads-up, you have to play accordingly, since you may be splitting the pot and your opponent may have a draw at you. Remember, getting three-quartered happens very often, and you must pay a lot of attention to this. So when you hold what looks like a big hand but there are many possibilities the other way, you must plan for these possibilities and determine the best way to deal with them. It often may be correct to check a hand, even though it looks like the best hand at that moment, because many cards can come to beat you.

For example, in a two-handed pot, you start with

and the flop is

Even though you have the nuts for high and no low is yet made, if your opponent plays back at you, you could be against the same high hand as you hold, plus a low draw. In this situation, you want to check and call on fourth street, no matter what hits. (Also notice that very few cards can come on fourth street that won't look scary.)

When the game becomes five-handed or less, which often happens when two or three players are walking or eating, most people at the table will continue to play along the same lines. That is, they won't adjust their game. They will be waiting on an ace-deuce and still will want four big cards suited up. In other words, they will play just as though the game were full.

So when the game becomes short-handed, you can begin to steal a lot of blinds. Most opponents will give up their blinds, as they have not adjusted to a short-handed game. You can play a lot more hands in this situation, plus you can maneuver many opponents because they will tend to go out. Also, since the pots won't be very big, the typical player will not want to go too far with his hand. In addition, he usually will play cautiously and try to conserve his chips until the game fills up again.

Scare Cards

Watch out for a player who has been calling and standing all bets and raises, and then suddenly starts betting and/or raising on the turn or the river when a scare card appears. You can be sure that either he had the nuts the whole way and was playing tricky or he just made the best hand. When this happens, especially if the last card could have made the nuts for either high or low, you probably will have to go out — no matter how big the pot is — and accept your loss. It is just too unlikely that your opponent would have called all the way in a jammed pot and then change gears and come out betting and/or raising without the last card giving him the cinch.

With experience, this situation becomes obvious. That is, your opponent was drawing for the cinch and was successful in obtaining it. In a sense, it's as though his hand was turned over and exposed. You therefore have to trim your loss and get out, even though the pot may have become quite large. Believe me, you virtually will never be wrong in this situation. Here's an example. You start with

On fourth street, the board is

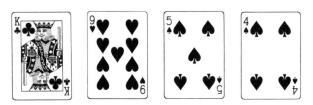

and the last card is the

If a player who has been just calling all along now bets and the pot is subsequently raised by another player who isn't likely to be going low, you easily could be against the nut flush as well as the nut low.

By the way, just because a scare card comes — not a key scare card that makes all the hands, but a card that might make some hands that can beat the hand you have — doesn't mean that you must check and give up all the bets on the end. Some players tend to do this every time a card comes that no longer gives them the cinch, even though they had the nuts and still hold close to the nuts.

For example, suppose the last card given in the illustration was the 8♣ instead of the 8♠. In this case, even though someone may have made a straight with a seven-six, automatically throwing away your hand is completely wrong, because the probability of the bets coming from only low hands has increased.

In these spots, you often are better off to go ahead and bet. If you get raised or the action becomes strong against you, then you can give it up. At least you discovered with certainty that you are beat without losing too much.

Most of the time, a typical player will be afraid that this scare card helped your hand and frequently will go out. This is especially true if the situation arises on fourth street. Now your opponent won't stay around and possibly catch a card that will beat you. Thus, a scary — but not too scary — card often can help you, even though it does not improve your hand. However, remember that if the card is very scary and many players are in the pot, you probably are beat and your best course of action is to throw away your hand.

Getting Counterfeited

You frequently get counterfeited in Omaha eight-or-better, even with tremendously big hands. For example, in a multiway pot, suppose you hold

and the flop comes

You have three aces, plus a wheel, which is the nut low that can't be counterfeited. Notice that you currently also have the best possible high hand with the wheel, and the three aces give you the best possible draw at an even better high hand.

Next, let's suppose that there is a great deal of jamming both on the flop and fourth street, meaning that some other players also have wheels. However, you are still in pretty good shape. Now on the river, a four or five hits, giving someone a six-high straight, and you get quartered or perhaps get less than that.

These types of hands come up fairly often, and you just have to live with them. You must realize that a lot of cards can come out that will counterfeit some great hands, and usually in a big multiway pot, people are drawing to beat these hands.

Thus, when you are in a position where you can get quartered and you are not playing for the whole pot, remember that the situation can change very quickly. You must consider this when deciding how to play your hand.

Getting Quartered

Even though you won't have many opportunities in Omaha eight-or-better to make great plays, when you have the chance to knock out someone who is drawing to the same hand that you are, you generally should try to do so. It is of utmost importance either to knock out an opponent who has the same hand that you have or to discard your hand when you are likely to be in this situation. Since you are splitting a lot of pots, you want to play in such a way that you avoid getting quartered.

It is easiest to gauge when someone has the same low hand that you have, such as an ace-deuce or an ace-trey. It is slightly harder to ascertain if you and an opponent both have the same high hand. But you often can get an idea, and if you suspect that both you and someone else are going in the same direction and trying to make the same hand, then you should either make a play designed to eliminate your opponent or fold if you don't think you can get him out of the pot.

To continue on but not eliminate this person is one of the worst disasters in this game. Always keep in mind that trying to win only one-quarter of the pot is *not* a winning strategy.

For example, if you hold just an ace-deuce and there is a lot of multiway action early, someone else also has an ace-deuce. Consequently, you probably should fold your hand, except when you have other winning draws working. These additional cards may include a suited ace, another low card, or a high pair. Notice that I am now describing a hand where the cards are working together in more than one way, which could make it a premium hand.

It is difficult to knock out someone who has an ace-deuce draw by raising into him. However, if someone raises into you, you probably should get out, as you are now trying to win only one-quarter of the pot if you make the low hand. Typical players will call the raise cold and then often find themselves quartered when the hand is over. In other words, they generally are committed to the pot. However, some of the good players know to fold, especially if the pot is raised and reraised.

Playing Against Steamers

Since they take numerous tough beats in Omaha eight-or-better, some of the high-stakes players will turn into steamers and start raising a lot. When steaming, the fairly good players will steam early in the hand. Before the flop — and to a lesser extent on the flop — is where they tend to raise or reraise when they shouldn't.

However, late in the hand, although some of these players might call too much, they usually won't be raising or putting a lot of action in the pot, because they are still aware that it is too easy to look at a cinch hand. So you have to remember that even though some players are steaming, if they bet later in the hand, they usually have the goods.

When players are steaming, their weaker low hands start to look better to them. This includes hands like

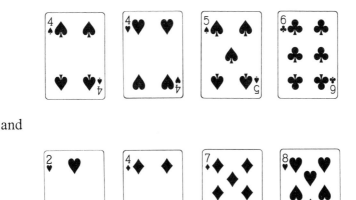

and

in multiway pots. (By the way, these hands rarely should be played.)

In most poker games, when you notice someone steaming, you generally want to raise to isolate him so you can play heads up. But in Omaha eight-or-better, this doesn't always do you as much good, because what hurts a weak hand the most is having many players against it.

By isolating an opponent, you are making his hand a lot closer in value to your hand, particularly if you hold a hand that can stand multiway action. So it doesn't pay to isolate a steamer who is a good player and who may now be playing basically high against you. You are better off most of the time to not reraise and to let other players in. This usually will devalue the steamer's hand, unless he happens to hold a big hand. Notice that you are getting your equity (even though it may be chopped up with some other players). However, it may be more equity for you if you happen to have the best hand anyway. This is especially true if you have several quality low cards.

If you hold a strictly high hand, you might be better off trying to isolate the steamer. But here you have to be careful, since you can get into trouble when other players call behind you, which usually will be the case if the game is loose.

Playing Against
Tight, Solid Players

In Omaha eight-or-better, you have to use all your reading skills to get a line on your opponents. You must observe the type of hands they play and how they play them.

Some people play only low hands, plus a few premium high hands with aces or perhaps four big cards suited up (and a few don't even play these hands). So when you come across players who won't play many — if any — high hands, and only one low card comes out on the flop, you frequently can win the pot either by bluffing them out or by having the best hand, even if it is a "trashy" hand.

In addition, consider position. Some players are very tight in early position but loosen up if they can come in late. This idea is important in most forms of poker, but in Omaha eight-or-better, it plays a major role.

To save money, don't give any action to those players who play very tight and very solid. There are usually a couple of them at every table, just grinding money by playing only the nuts, especially against weaker players. Late in the hand, if these tight players show any strength, don't play with them. They won't bet or raise unless they have you beat.

Early in the hands, even though hand values run fairly close, tight players tend to go out too much. That is, they sometimes won't even take another card off when it is correct to do so. Consequently, the biggest advantage you have against this type of player is not giving him any action later in the hand, unless you are sure that you have the best hand. Very tight, very solid players usually have either the nuts or at least a hand close to the nuts.

Even in pots that are quite large, if one of these players comes out betting or raising, or he is in there calling on a jammed hand, he almost always has the nuts for low and usually has some kind of nut draw for the high side. It just doesn't pay to stay in these pots.

However, you have the benefit of being able to easily spot this type of player. He is not in many pots, he does not raise very often, and on the end, he almost always shows the nuts when he turns over his hand. He may not win the whole pot and may even get quartered occasionally when he goes all the way. But, as just stated, he usually has a cinch. The few times that a tight, solid player goes to the end and then throws away his hand, he has missed a big draw. His body language generally indicates that this was the case (he might make a face or squirm around in his chair), so you should be able to recognize him.

To repeat, it just doesn't pay to give these super-tight players any action. You might have to force yourself to discard your hand when you are against them, but you usually won't regret it. For example, if you play on the low side when they are going low, watch for an ace-deuce or an ace-deuce-trey in their hands. You are going to be quartering the pots with them, and frequently they have high hands to go with their superior low draws. As a result, you will be taking much the worst of it.

You often will have the advantage of knowing where they stand. But their hands are usually so strong that this doesn't help much, except for telling you to go out.

It is helpful for this type of player to be sitting on your right, because when he enters the pot, you will know to go out with all but your very best hands. In most other games, you generally want tight, unimaginative players on your left, as you can raise them out of pots. Even when you don't raise, they seldom get in your way. But in Omaha eight-or-better, they do get in your way. Thus, it is better to have them on your right where they act first, so you know whether or not they will play.

If three or four tight players happen to be sitting in a row, you probably would prefer to have them across from you rather than on your immediate right. If they are sitting to your immediate right and are out of most pots, you will find yourself playing many hands out of position with the looser players on your left.

The very tight, solid players cause you to maneuver in and out of hands according to where the blind hits in relation to them. You will have to consider how many of them are in the game and where everyone else is positioned. But if only one or two of these super-tight players are in the game and you have a chance to get them on your immediate right, by all means change seats and do so.

Another benefit of having tight, unimaginative players on your right is that as the game becomes short-handed, they won't adjust. Thus, they will be out of a lot of pots and you will be able to play many hands against the blinds, which is a big advantage.

Also, when you are in the blind, tight players will be in the attack position but will do very little stealing. Consequently, you won't have to defend when one of these players raises, because he will have a premium hand. In addition, you may get some walks (that is, win the pot when no one plays) or not be raised, which allows you to play a poor hand and perhaps get lucky.

Finally, if the little blind just calls, he is a very tight, solid player, and you have position with the big blind, you can raise and frequently outplay him. This is another small advantage to having this type of opponent on your right.

When a tight, solid player is situated on your immediate left, you ordinarily could steal the blind from him. But in Omaha eight-or-better, unless the game is very tight, it seldom happens that you are on the button and no one else comes in. (Incidentally, if the game is this tight, you probably should look for another game.)

However, when the game is tight, players in front of the button often will all pass. So it might do you some good to have the really tight players on your left. It is also OK to have bad players on your left in an extremely tight game. Since position is so important, if they enter the pot when you have the button, there are a lot of different ways that you can win.

Nevertheless, keep in mind that if you are going to make any real money in Omaha eight-or-better, you are not going to do it stealing blinds. You will have to get played with somewhere along the line, and it might as well be against weaker players.

Your Playing Style

If you are the kind of player who prefers to play tight and you pride yourself on making good laydowns, getting out of pots, and not getting squeezed in, then your strategy most of the time is to just call, keep the pot small early, and get out early in the hand without making crucial mistakes.

However, when you are playing in a game where a lot of the pots get raised early, many of your laydowns will be wrong. Some of these laydowns not only will be costly, but also may turn you into a losing player.

If you are a player who usually knows where he stands, it doesn't hurt to build the pots and lock your opponents into their hands. This will allow you to punish them late in the hand in jammed pots by making them put in extra money when they have the worst of it. Even though your edge will be smaller per unit bet, there will be more units bet.

If you are an aggressive player and have a good feel for the game, you can build the pots a lot sooner. In addition, you will prefer to play in tight games, especially against opponents who are easy to maneuver.

If you tend to call too much, then you are better off building the pots early — or trying to induce them to be built early — so that on the later rounds, your mistakes won't be as critical. However, if you know you call too much, you should try to call less. Reining in your compulsion to call may be difficult, as not everyone has complete control over himself. Only the very best do, and even they slip occasionally.

If you are a timid, passive player who wants to play only the nuts, you probably should push your hands more than you normally do. If you get lost in a hand, you should consider betting anyway, because you generally will be playing with a strong hand, and strong hands tend to do well.

If you are a weak player who plays too loose and calls too much, you shouldn't be playing Omaha eight-or-better. In fact, you should drop down to smaller stakes and contemplate playing seven-card stud. Although weak, loose players usually lose in both games, you will have a slightly better chance in stud.

Most players should find a game that is suited to their individual instincts and styles. Very aggressive players are better off playing limit hold 'em or seven-card stud, and less aggressive players are better off playing split-type games. So you should try to recognize exactly what your style is and select a game tailored to that style.

Fluctuations

Since Omaha eight-or-better has a lot of redraws, and since the pots often get jammed in aggressive games — especially on some of the later rounds — the fluctuations can be quite large at the higher limits. Accordingly, you want to have the proper amount of chips to play for each session, as you can go through some major swings.

However, it will seem as though your chips really don't fluctuate that much. This is a funny quirk of Omaha eight-or-better. In fact, often you may think you have fairly good control of your chips. But in reality, this is seldom true. What happens is that the game is very slow; it takes a long time to play a hand and a long time to split the pot. In addition, people spend a lot of time thinking in this game, since it is easy to get lost in a hand. This is especially true for those players who tag along with weak hands. Their pauses do not necessarily indicate that they are thinking about making a play, but that they are trying to determine if they have enough chance of winning half the pot to make it worthwhile to continue playing. This is sometimes a reliable tell, unless they are deceptive players. By the way, the slow player is usually the person getting chopped up in the hand.

Because Omaha eight-or-better is such a slow game, in the course of a night, you play a lot fewer hands than in other games. So you are not stacking as many pots, and your chips do not seem to be going up and down as much. However, they are going up and down a lot more per hand played rather than according to time spent at the table.

Pot-Limit
Omaha Eight-or-Better

Pot-limit Omaha eight-or-better is still frequently played. Basically, a winning strategy in this game boils down to selecting the same kind of hands, except for added emphasis on the high hands, hands with redraws to still better hands, and high hands that can back into lows.

Most of the time, the pots are raised and reraised fairly early in the hand, and the play becomes heads up. In this case, high hands will take the majority of the money if played properly, and high hands that also have low possibilities, as well as flush potential, are exceptionally good. Thus, if you get outdrawn on the turn, you still can win half the pot or possibly redraw for high.

Bluffing in a limit game is fairly futile, unless you are heads up or the game is very tight. In looser games, there is little bluffing, with the possible exception of making a bet or a raise to slow down the action on a later round. However, in a pot-limit game, the bluff comes up frequently, since you can raise or check-raise someone's bet three times, assuming that he bets the pot. Also, betting the size of the pot makes it tougher to chase with a marginal hand. Consequently, you will need much stronger hands to play as the pots get bet and raised. You almost always will get poor odds to try and draw out. So if you don't have the best hand, chasing is usually wrong. As a result, pot-limit Omaha eight-or-better is probably a dying game, because the players who play too loose will get cut up too much and too fast. They won't catch enough miracle cards to survive.

When playing pot-limit, the check-raise is very strong. By check-raising, you can raise a lot more and shut someone out of the pot a lot easier than by just betting. Sometimes it may not even be necessary to have the best low, since you might be able to drive out the best low. Your check-raise could force the player

258

with the nut low to put his whole stack in if he wants to play, and he may think he will get quartered.

If you have a low hand and check, the player with the other likely low will check, the likely high hand will bet, and you can check-raise. A good player will fold, since it looks as though you also may have the nut low. In fact, he will know to do this, because he does not want to put all his money in and get quartered.

In a limit game, it is difficult to knock out someone in this spot, although you sometimes should try it. The most likely exception is early in the hand when there is not much money in the pot. The better players will be more inclined to fold.

Thus, pot-limit Omaha eight-or-better affords a few more bluffing opportunities, which add to the skills required to be successful. But the game should play much tighter, and of course position becomes even stronger. This includes not only position in relation to the button, but also — and even more important — position during the hand as you fall in relation to both the high and the low hands.

Additional
Advanced Concepts

Afterthought

You must understand how to play your hand for maximum profit. Sometimes this means to fold, since folding and winning zero is better than getting quartered or worse. This is why having extra draws is so important, especially if the game is loose.

In heads-up play, the opposite can be true. Now you don't necessarily need that good of a hand. You want position, and you want to be against a weak opponent.

You also need to understand the significance of scary cards in multiway pots. A scare card often indicates that you should discard a fairly good hand that might have been the nuts on the previous street. But if the card is only slightly scary, you frequently should pay off the bet in a large pot.

Also remember that in Omaha eight-or-better, unlike in many other forms of poker, you generally don't want to isolate the steamers. Even though they probably have poor hands, they are not always in that bad of shape when they are heads up. In addition, make sure that you save money against the tight, solid players. It is just not worth giving these people any action. When they bet or raise, they typically have the best hand.

Finally, keep in mind that in some of the more aggressive games, especially if they are fairly loose, you can go through some big swings. At the lower limits, those of you who play tight can get by with a relatively small bankroll. But this won't necessarily be true at the higher limits, even though the slow speed of the game sometimes will make you think that you have fairly good control.

Part Four

Other Skills

Other Skills

Introduction

There are two additional areas that play a major role in winning at Omaha eight-or-better (as well as at all forms of poker). They are reading hands and psychology.

Reading hands is both an art and a science. The same is true for correct applications of psychology at the poker table. In both instances, you must know your opponents. More specifically, the better you understand how your opponents think and thus how they play, the better you will be able to choose the correct strategies to use against them.

When you are not in a pot, it is still very important to pay attention to what is going on. By doing so, you will begin to understand how different opponents play their hands in different situations and what tactics they are most likely to try. Also, you can get a feel for how they think. You will notice what they handle easily and what confuses them, and you will get an idea of what strategies work best against them.

Keep in mind that the concepts discussed in this section cannot be mastered quickly. Like many other skills at the Omaha eight-or-better table, reading hands and applying psychology take a while to learn. But once mastered, they will become significant factors in your winning play. And for those of you who make it to the very big games (and perhaps compete against the world champions), you must become an expert in these two areas to have any chance of success.

Reading Hands

Excellent techniques are available for reading hands in Omaha eight-or-better. Most commonly, you analyze the meaning of an opponent's check, bet, or raise, and you look at the exposed cards and try to judge from them what his entire hand might be. You then combine the plays he has made *throughout the hand* with the exposed cards and come to a determination about his most likely hand.

In other words, you use logic to read hands. You interpret your opponents' plays on each round and note the cards that appear on the board, paying close attention to the order in which they appear. You then put these two pieces of evidence together — the plays and the cards on the board — to draw a conclusion about an opponent's most likely hand.

Sometimes you can put an opponent on a specific hand quite early. However, in general, it's a mistake to do this and then stick to your initial conclusion no matter how things develop. A player who raises before the flop and then raises again after two high cards have flopped may have made a set, but he also may be on a draw and is trying for a free card. Drawing a narrow, irreversible conclusion early can lead to costly mistakes later, such as giving that free card or betting into your opponent when he makes his hand.

What you should do is to put an opponent on a variety of hands at the start of play, and as play progresses, eliminate some of those hands based on his later play and on the cards that come. Through this process of elimination, you should have a good idea of what this opponent has (or is drawing to) when the last card is dealt.

For instance, suppose that before the flop, an opponent calls after you raise. On the flop, two small cards appear, as well as two suited cards, and he raises after you bet. An offsuit eight then comes on the turn, but when you check to him, he also checks. It is now likely that this player is on a flush draw — probably the nut flush draw — and was buying a free card. If a flush card comes on the river, you should not bet into him. In addition, if the flush card does not hit, you may want to check on the end and call, hoping to induce a bluff. However, if you have only a low made and cannot beat even a weak high, you may want to bet, since there is a reasonable chance that you can pick up the whole pot.

At the end of a hand, it becomes especially crucial to have a good idea of what your opponent has. The more accurately you can read hands, the better you can determine what your chances are of having your opponent beat. This, of course, helps you in deciding how to play your hand.

In practice, most players at least try to determine whether an opponent has a bad hand, a mediocre hand, a good hand, or a great hand. For instance, let's say your opponent bets on the end. Usually when a person bets, it represents a bluff, a good hand, or a great hand, but not a mediocre hand. If your opponent had a mediocre hand, he probably would check. If you have only a mediocre hand, you must determine what the chances are that your opponent is bluffing and whether those chances warrant a call in relation to the pot odds. For example, most players will not bet on the end with a low that isn't the nuts, especially if they are against several opponents. They hope to win in a showdown with this mediocre hand.

One way to read hands is to start by considering possible cards that an opponent might have and then to eliminate some of those possibilities as the hand develops. A complementary way to read hands is to work backward. For instance, if someone cold calls a raise and a reraise before the flop, the flop comes

the fourth-street card is the

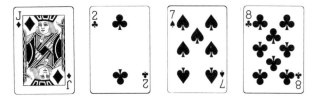

and he is able to raise on fourth street, you think back to his play in earlier rounds. Since it does not seem possible that your opponent would have called on the flop if he had something like a three-card low or a big pair smaller than aces before the flop, you now have to suspect that he has made a set of aces.

Here is another example. Suppose on fourth street that the board is

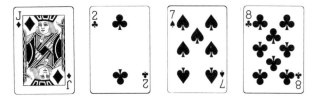

The pot is multiway, and one player called a raise before the flop, called the bet on the flop, and now raises. What is his hand?

First, notice it is unlikely that this player just has the nut low, even though it is probable that he started with an ace-trey. Since the pot is being contested multiway, he would fear that he might get quartered. This is why he only called on the flop. On the turn, he still should be afraid of being quartered, and since a straight card hit, he would not have raised if he had a set. However, he could have the nut low and a draw at the nut flush. So even though he might get quartered, he also may be able to hog the whole pot if a club hits. There is a good chance that he holds the ace of clubs, as well as a trey and another club.

Now for a third example. Before the flop, several people limp in, and the pot is then raised by a player in late position. On the flop, two high cards and two diamonds fall. One of the original limpers, who is in an early position, bets and gets several callers between him and the before-the-flop raiser. If the before-the-flop raiser now raises again, there is a good chance that he has the nut flush draw. This would be especially true if he is not the type of player who likes to get a lot of money in the pot before the flop with a high hand. Consequently, if the before-the-flop raiser plays his high hands fast, it would be conceivable for him to have made a big set. In fact, this hand would now be more likely than the flush draw.

When you can't actually put a person on a hand but have reduced his possible holdings to a limited number, you try to use mathematics to determine the chances of his having certain hands rather than others. Then you decide what kind of hand you must have to continue playing.

Sometimes you can use a mathematical procedure based on Bayes' Theorem to determine the chances that an opponent has one hand or another. After deciding on the kinds of hands your opponent would be betting in a particular situation, you determine the probability of your opponent holding each of those hands. Then you compare the probabilities.

Here's an example. Suppose an extremely loose and aggressive opponent just calls before the flop. Two high cards flop — which gives you top set — you bet and he calls. On fourth street, an ace hits, which could make a straight, and this player bets into you. You now must decide whether you should raise or just call. Since your opponent is a loose aggressive player, he is not likely to have made three aces, as he would have raised before the flop. But he is likely to be betting a hand like aces up. Therefore, you should raise. If you get reraised, meaning that you are probably against a straight, you have a lot of outs to improve. On the other hand, if your opponent is tighter and more conservative, he is much more likely to have the straight. Now you should just call.

Knowing it is slightly more likely that your opponent has one kind of holding versus another does not always tell you how you should proceed in the play of your hand. Nevertheless, the more you know about the chances of an opponent having one hand rather than another when he bets or raises, the easier it is for you to decide whether to fold, call, or raise.

Here's another example. Suppose you start with

You raise, and an opponent behind you reraises. The flop comes king high. You check and your opponent bets. If you think your opponent is as likely to have a hand like ace-deuce-trey as he is to have a pair of aces, you should at least call. If an ace hits on a later street and your opponent bets again, you may want to raise if you know this opponent would still bet if he had only two aces. This is because it is now much more mathematically likely that you have the best hand.

Finally, as this last example shows, you need to complement mathematical conclusions with what you know about a player. For instance, players almost always will just call if they make a quality low on the flop and will try to raise you on a later street. If a player calls on the flop and then raises on fourth or fifth street after irrelevant cards hit, he is much more likely to have a quality low than he is to have made a set with one of the seemingly irrelevant cards.

Another factor in reading hands and deciding how to play your own hand is the number of players in the pot. People tend to play their hands much more straightforwardly in multiway pots. This is also true when several players are yet to act. So if a player bets in either of these situations, you can be quite sure that he's got a real hand.

Psychology

What I mean by "the psychology of poker" is getting into your opponents' heads, analyzing how they think, figuring out what they think you think, and even determining what they think you think they think. In this sense, the psychology of poker is an extension of reading opponents' hands. It is also an extension of using deception in the way you play your own hand.

Here's an example. Before the flop, you raise from late position with a weak hand, trying to steal the blinds. You get reraised by a strong player behind you, who knows you automatically would attempt to steal in this position. Since you know that he knows you automatically would try to steal, his reraise does not mean that he has a very good hand. Consequently, because your opponent might also be bluffing, the correct play may be for you to raise back and then to bet again on fourth and fifth streets if necessary.

This brings up another point. The above play works because you are against a strong player whose thinking makes sense. A weak player is a different story. Just as you can't put a weak player on a hand, you can't put him on a thought either.

Very sophisticated Omaha eight-or-better can go even beyond this third level. For example, two small cards flop, an early position player (who raised coming in) bets, and a strong player calls. A blank hits on fourth street, and the player in early position bets again. His opponent, who thinks this player is probably on a low draw (perhaps because he knows this player is reluctant to play high hands up front), may now raise with only top pair. His opponent may realize this and raise back, trying to represent a strong hand. The initial raiser now may comprehend this possibility and call his opponent down. When the hand is over, assuming that the low card does not come, if the initial raiser is actually against a low draw, his calls will look fantastic to some opponents. Conversely, if it turns out that the first bettor really has a hand, the calls will look like a "sucker play."

At the expert level of Omaha eight-or-better, the "skill" of trying to outwit your opponent sometimes can extend to so many levels that your judgment may begin to fail. However, in ordinary play against good players, you should think at least up to the third level. First, think about what your opponent has. Second, think about what your opponent thinks you have. And third, think about what your opponent thinks you think he has. Only when you are playing against weak players, who might not bother to think about what you have and who almost certainly don't think about what you think they have, does it not necessarily pay to go through such thought processes. Against all others, this is crucial to successful play, since deception is a big part of the game.

Several other important ideas play major roles in the psychology of poker. To begin with, when an opponent bets in a situation where he is sure that you are going to call, he is not bluffing. For example, suppose you have been betting all the way, you bet again after all the cards are out, and a player raises you. It is rare to find an opponent who is capable of raising on the end as a bluff. Similarly, if you raise when all the cards are out and your opponent reraises, you usually should fold, unless your hand can beat some of the legitimate hands with which he might be raising or you have a lock for one side. (Even though you could get quartered, your call still may be correct because of the size of the pot.) But beware of the player who knows you are capable of these folds.

However, folding is not necessarily correct on fourth street. Tough players will raise on this street if they hold a mediocre hand that has some potential of becoming a very strong hand. An example is a draw at the second nut low that also has picked up a flush draw. Those of you who fold when raised in these situations are giving up too much. This is especially true at the larger limits, where the games are usually tougher and these plays are more common.

A corollary to the principle that we are discussing is that if your opponent bets when there appears to be a good chance that you will fold, he may very well be bluffing. What this means in practice is that if your opponent bets in a situation where he thinks he might be able to get away with a bluff, you have to give more consideration to calling him, even with a mediocre hand.

An example is when no one bets on fourth street, a small pair and two high cards are on board, and another small card hits on the river. If one of your opponents now bets, and he is the type of player who would try to pick up the pot with nothing, it may be correct for you to call or raise with a weak hand.

In deciding whether to bet, it is equally important to consider what your opponent thinks you have. If your opponent suspects a strong hand, you should bluff more. However, you should not bet a fair hand for value in this situation.

An example is when you raise on the flop, which shows two suited cards and only one small card, and a blank hits on fourth street. If you check on fourth street but bet again on the river when a third suited card lands, it is difficult for many opponents to call with less than a flush. So bet your weaker hands in this spot.

Conversely, if you know your opponent suspects that you are weak, you should not try to bluff, as you will get caught. But you should bet your fair hands for value. As an example, if both you and your opponent checked on fourth street, you frequently can bet two pair on the end for value.

Varying your play and making an "incorrect" play intentionally are also part of the psychology of Omaha eight-or-better, because you are trying to affect the thinking of your opponents for future hands. Before the flop, for example, you occasionally can reraise a late-position player, who may be on a steal, when you hold something like deuce-trey for low and two face cards. Assuming that your opponents see your hand in a showdown, they should be less inclined to steal against you in a similar situation. Also, you are taking advantage of the impression you created to get paid off later when you bet with a legitimate reraising hand.

Another example of this type of play is to throw in an extra raise early with a hand that doesn't really warrant it in order to give the *illusion of action*. For instance, before the flop, you occasionally can reraise a raiser with a hand like

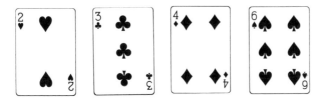

especially if you are going to play this holding anyway. This play costs only a fraction of a bet in mathematical expectation but gains you a tremendous amount in future action on subsequent hands.

There are also other ways to affect your opponents' play on future hands in Omaha eight-or-better. For example, you may want to make what you think is a bad call if you believe this play will keep other players from running over you. If you find that you have been forced to throw away your hand on the end two or three times in a row, you must be prepared to call the next time with a hand that you normally wouldn't call with. This is because you can assume that your opponents have noticed your folding and are apt to try to bluff you.

Another less obvious situation where you should think of the future is to check in early position on the flop with a high hand, such as

and then check again on fourth street, even if you got a flop you liked. Not only may you catch someone stealing, but this check also might allow you to steal the pot yourself in a future hand when there has been almost no betting on the early rounds (especially when an irrelevant card hits the board). You can get away with a steal because you have shown your opponents that you are capable of checking a big hand twice. Thus someone with a mediocre hand may not call the double-sized bet.

In general, you should evaluate any play you make on its merits alone, that is, on its expectation in a given situation. However, you occasionally might want to do something that is theoretically incorrect to create an impression for the future. Once you have opponents thinking one way, you can take advantage of that thinking later.

Finally, keep in mind that these types of plays will work against opponents who are good enough to try to take advantage of their new-found knowledge, but who are not good enough to realize that you know this and that they should therefore ignore it. In Omaha eight-or-better, as in all poker games, there seems to be a large group of players who like to "realize things." You must know how these people think and whether they are thinking only on the level that you are giving them credit for. If they think on a still higher level, you have to step up to that level.

Other Skills

Afterthought

As you have just seen, reading hands and psychology are extremely important aspects of Omaha eight-or-better. Put another way, this game is too complex to play by rote at the higher limits. If you always play a certain hand in a certain position a certain way, your game can use a lot of improvement. You must take into account your opponents, how the current hand has been played, how former hands were played, your opponents' perceptions of you, and so on. If you don't consider these things, you may be able to win, but you never will achieve expert status.

Many of the concepts in this section are most powerful against decent players — that is, players who play in predictable patterns and who are capable of realizing things when at the poker table. Against bad players, straightforward play is usually the best approach, and against extremely good players, these ideas probably will keep you only about even with them.

Finally, some players put too much emphasis on the topics just covered. They are certainly very important, but they are just some of the weapons that the expert has in his Omaha eight-or-better arsenal. To produce a top player, reading hands and psychology must be utilized in conjunction with all the other ideas and concepts that I have addressed.

Part Five

Questions and Answers

Questions and Answers

Introduction

A great deal of material has been covered in this book. However, for many people, reading and learning can be two different things. Consequently, to help you retain some of the more significant ideas, I have reiterated them in a question-and-answer format.

I suggest that after you have read and studied this text, you try to answer the following questions. You probably will want to go over them many times. In addition, I recommend that you cover the answer that immediately follows each question. Only look at the solution after you have answered the question to the best of your ability. Since many of the questions are general in nature, this will make you think back on what you should have learned.

Also, I want to point out that what follows is not a substitute for the text. In fact, many of the ideas in the book are not contained here. But enough material is included so that after you have thoroughly digested the text, the questions should help keep your Omaha eight-or-better game sharp.

Finally, the questions and answers are organized by topics covered in the text, so you can easily return to the appropriate section for a fuller explanation.

Note: The questions in this section and the next section refer to the low-limit games, where the strategy is fairly straightforward.

General Concepts

1. When playing in the lower limits, there are two kinds of games. What are they?

   The first type is a game in which people are playing too loosely, especially after the flop; the second is a game where the players generally know what they are doing.

2. What is the main error that players make in the first type of game?

   They draw to hands that are not the nuts.

3. Where does your primary edge come from in these games?

   After the flop, you will draw only to the nuts for low and only to hands that have an excellent chance of being a sure winner for high.

4. In games where people play approximately correctly, what must you do?

   You must play not only correctly on the flop but also very tightly before the flop.

5. In low-limit Omaha eight-or-better, is there an advantage to being simply the tightest player both before the flop and on the flop?

   Yes, as this will ensure you a significant edge.

6. But what if the game is fairly good?

   You will cost yourself a lot of profit if you play too tightly before the flop.

7. Suppose you have ace-deuce and the game is reasonably tough?
   In this situation, your ace-deuce loses most of its profitability, since other players won't be drawing to the second and third nuts as often.

8. Suppose you have a low draw and someone bets. What might you need to do?
   Raise to squeeze another player off a low draw. (This works against only a few good players.)

9. What should you sometimes do before the flop?
   Reraise to knock out players behind you so that you are last to act.

10. What is your primary objective?
    To play hands that can develop into two-way hands, where you can either scoop or three-quarter an opponent.

11. Suppose you have A♠2♣6♦7♦. How should you play?
    You may wish to raise, because you don't want someone holding a hand like 6♥7♣8♦9♠ to also play in a multiway pot.

12. Why do you want this player out?
    Because he can make a higher straight than you can make, plus you can get quartered by tying for the low with some other players.

13. What hands tend to do really well in this game?
    Hands containing ace-deuce and ace-deuce-trey.

14. What else is beneficial?
    Having a suited card with the ace.

15. What about four high cards?
    In many spots, they also do well, because if this hand wins, there probably will not be a low.

16. What about three big cards that include an ace, plus a deuce or a trey?
    They are also good hands.

17. What if two low cards hit the board?
    All high hands go way down in value.

More Specific Ideas

1. Should you play middle-sized cards, such as 4♦5♥6♥7♣?
   No.

2. Why not?
   Because you can't make the nuts, barring an occasional exception.

3. Why is a hand like 6♥7♦8♣9♠ quite a bit worse than a hand like 10♣J♠Q♥K♦?
   Because if you make the nut straight, the low is out there.

4. Should you always play two aces?
   No. A pair of aces with nothing else going for it generally should be thrown away in early position.

5. What if there is no raising?
   You can call with a weak two-ace hand, hoping to hit your set.

6. When would you throw away a hand that has an ace-deuce with nothing else?
   Against tight players for a cold raise.

7. What about a weak ace-trey in early position?
   It usually will cost you money.

8. Is there an exception?
   Yes, when the game has one or more extremely live players.

9. What about four low cards without an ace, such as 2♥3♦4♣5♥?
   Hands like this are not so bad, because if an ace hits, your lows are good.

10. Suppose you play one of these hands, the pot is multiway, and no ace flops?

Usually you should throw away your hand, but it depends on exactly what comes out.

11. Is there a big difference between ace-trey and deuce-trey?

Yes. In good position, ace-trey is almost always worth playing before the flop, but deuce-trey is usually not.

12. What about high pairs with two other big cards?

They generally are playable.

13. What is a problem with flopping a set of aces?

The ace puts a low card on board.

14. Does this mean that you should play two kings stronger than two aces?

No, as an ace could come to beat you.

15. Suppose you hold a hand like K♠K♦Q♣J♥. Should you raise before the flop?

No. Most of the preflop raising in this game is done strictly to knock out players behind you.

16. What about raising before the flop to get more money in the pot?

This is normally not the best strategy.

17. When would you generally go ahead and raise?

When you hold a hand like A♠A♦2♣3♦.

18. What about position?

It is very important, and you can play more hands in the late positions than in the early positions. However, you still shouldn't play the medium-sized hands.

19. How does a lot of raising before the flop affect you?

    It adds marginally to your profits, but it adds tremendously to your fluctuations.

20. Does a lot of raising before the flop affect the number of hands that you should play?

    Not much. You still should play almost the same number of hands.

21. There is an exception. What is it?

    You should throw away the marginal hands that you sometimes can play in late position.

22. How do large pots affect your play on the flop?

    You are forced to play slightly looser. For example, you might go for a back-door low with an ace-deuce if you have something else, such as a back-door nut flush draw.

23. Give an example of a trap hand on the flop.

    The flop is 5♠6♠9♥, and you have a trey-four with a jack-high flush draw. You should discard this hand if you are against several opponents.

24. What if you are heads up?

    You might play this hand, unless you are against someone who won't gamble.

25. In general, what kind of hands do you want to play?

    Those hands that can make the nuts.

26. What is a common exception?

    You are heads up and the hand has many different possibilities.

27. How do completed low hands affect the high hands?
    Completed low hands cause high hands to lose most of their value.

28. What does having back-door potential or a lot of outs do for you?
    Either may make your hand playable.

29. Give an example.
    You have A♠K♠K♥3♦, and the flop comes 10♠8♥4♣. Even though you are drawing to only a deuce for the nut low, a king may win the whole pot for you, and another spade gives you the nut flush draw.

30. What if you make an ace-trey low?
    You have to decide whether you should pay off a bet.

31. What if you are caught in a jam?
    You should throw away your hand.

32. Suppose you are going low on the flop. How should you usually play your hand?
    Cautiously, unless you can't get counterfeited, you have an ace-high flush draw, or you have other potential.

33. What if you flop top set?
    You don't mind going to war if there is no low draw and you are against a maniac type player who easily could have a smaller set.

34. What if you make your low but are sure that you are getting quartered?
    You may have to throw away your hand.

35. Example?

> You have an ace-deuce. The flop comes 5♣6♦7♠, you are last to act, and five opponents ahead of you are betting, raising, and reraising. In this situation, you probably should discard your hand.

36. When you play an ace-trey in a multiway pot and flop a low draw, what should you often do?

> Throw away your hand, especially if you have nothing else to go with your low draw.

37. Give an example of a bluffing opportunity.

> The flop comes 10♦9♠3♣, and there is a bet. You sometimes can raise with virtually nothing. In a short-handed pot, your opponent might have bet an ace-ten figuring that you have nothing.

38. Suppose you have an ace-deuce, have made your low on fourth street, but have nothing else to go with it. How should you play your hand if there is a bet and a couple of callers?

> Just call. You don't want the original bettor to reraise and knock out the players in the middle.

39. Suppose the initial bettor is a tight player who almost always goes for low, and you have a medium pair to go along with your low?

> Now if he reraises and knocks out everyone else, you might win the high.

40. Do you raise on the end when you have the nuts?

> Not necessarily. It is sometimes correct to check it down.

41. Example?

> You are last to act in a four-person pot, and the board is 2♦3♠4♣5♦J♦. If all you have is a wheel, you are probably against one or perhaps two other wheels, as well as a flush.

42. You have an ace-deuce. How does play in a four-handed pot differ from play in a three-handed pot?

> If someone else also has an ace-deuce, you lose money by raising in a three-handed pot. Thus you should not raise. In a four-handed pot, you would break even. So now you can raise.

43. What are the exceptions to not raising in a three-handed pot?

> You play well and are fairly sure that you are not against another ace-deuce, or you are against an opponent who is extremely live.

Note: The rest of the questions refer to the high-limit games, where the strategy is much more complex. You will be playing against many players who are highly skilled and expect to have good results. You also must play very well.

General Concepts

1. What should you normally try to do before the flop?
   Get in cheaply.

2. Why would you put in a lot of money early?
   Usually to knock out players so you have a positional advantage.

3. What is the big decision?
   To analyze the flop and understand how it relates to your hand and whether you should play on.

4. What do most people do in this game?
   They tend to play too loose after the flop.

5. When a lot of players take the flop, what must you have to continue?
   The nut low draw, the nut low made *with redraws*, or a very strong high hand.

6. What is one of the big skill factors in this game?
   Understanding how the other players play their hands and playing your hand accordingly.

7. What is the secret of this game?
   To have the nuts with draws to better hands.

8. What does this mean?

That it is important to have all four of your cards working well together so you have back-door possibilities.

9. What will this sometimes allow you to do?

To take some pots back or, at times, to three-quarter your opponent instead of splitting the pot.

Position

1. Do you play many hands up front?

No, as there is too much jamming.

2. What does this mean?

That you should play only the absolute premium hands in early position.

3. What if the game is tight?

You will want to play few hands up front and to steal a lot of pots in the back.

4. What if the game is loose?

Stealing becomes unimportant, as you virtually never have the opportunity to try it.

5. You still expect action when you attempt to steal from late position, so why do you want to play a lot of weaker hands from this spot?

Many players won't play without ace-deuce, ace-trey, or some other big hand. This means that you frequently will end up playing against the blinds, who will take a flop with a weak hand to see what is out there.

Low Hands

1. When many people have entered the pot, why is playing a hand that just contains ace-deuce or ace-trey not enough?
   Because you often will get quartered, unless your opponents are very bad players.

2. In multiway pots, what hands do you want?
   Hands that have a third low card, such as ace-deuce-trey or ace-deuce-four, or four low cards with the ace in your hand.

3. What often occurs in multiway pots?
   A lot of the low hands get counterfeited by one of your low cards coming out on fourth or fifth street.

4. How do you play tremendous low hands, such as three or four low cards that also might be suited up?
   You don't mind putting in more money early, because much of the time you will flop a low hand or a draw to a low hand.

5. How do you now play if a lot of money goes in early?
   You should take a card off to see fourth street, even when the flop is not very favorable.

6. What if high cards come early?
   There rarely will be more than one high hand with strength, so it is unlikely that you will get jammed.

7. What if low cards come?
   The high hand will get jammed in.

8. What is a general rule to remember?
   Jammed pots when low cards flop usually mean several low draws.

9. In medium- to high-stakes games, is an ace-deuce automatically a giant hand?

No, it is not the kind of hand to wait for.

10. Is this true at the low-stakes games?

No, as there are almost always players who consistently draw at the third and fourth (or even worse) low hands.

11. In a high-stakes game, when would you be more willing to play a dry ace-deuce?

When there is a "live one" in the pot.

High Hands

1. How do high hands perform in situations where no low card or only one comes on the flop?
    Well.

2. What if two or three low cards come on the flop?
    The high hands now do poorly.

3. In what type of games do high hands do well?
    In games where the pot is not raised before the flop.

4. Why?
    Because it is more likely than not that two low cards will flop, meaning that most flops are going to be unplayable.

5. Suppose you flop top set but two low cards are also on board?
    Your hand often will be in trouble, because low straights and flushes are fairly easy to make.

6. What does this mean?
    You want to play more high hands in games where it does not cost much to see the flop.

7. What if the action is not multiway?
    It doesn't matter whether you get in cheaply, because high hands play well short-handed.

8. Why do suited high hands do well in tight games?
    Because three low cards don't always appear. When they do come, they may not make your opponents' hands.

9. What do you want to avoid?

Playing when it looks as though other people might be counterfeiting your hand.

10. Example?

A hand like 10♠J♥Q♦K♠ is usually very good. But if a couple of other players also are playing high with similar big cards, your hand is probably somewhat counterfeited by their hands.

11. When do you want to have high hands?

When you are in a short-handed pot against players who play only the low hands.

12. In what situation do high hands not play well?

Against players who play extremely tight and are likely to have a hand like two aces with low cards.

13. Why is having a hand that can go further without much early improvement an advantage?

Because it has more opportunity for overall improvement. Also, your opponent can bet for value more often or bluff and knock you out when you would have had a winning hand at a later stage.

14. What must you do when playing the high hands heads up?

You must call a lot of times and see how the hand develops.

15. Why is this so?

Because you often will split the pot with a low hand.

16. But what if the board becomes real scary?

If a player shows strength, you will have to get out.

17. By reading your opponent, what should you be able to determine?

Whether you have a split or a probable loser.

18. What are some hints to help you in this area?
  1. Pay attention to the game.
  2. Try to understand the meaning of someone's bet, check, or raise. (Will your opponent make a play short-handed?)
  3. Is anyone currently steaming?
  4. When in a tough situation, take all the time you need to determine the best course of action.
  5. Spend time away from the table thinking about some of your tougher hands.

19. How should you play high hands when the flop is such that a lot of scare cards can come to beat you?

In this situation, you don't want to play high hands too aggressively.

20. When is this particularly true?

When you have flopped a set and the other two cards on board are reasonably close together.

21. Example?

You have Q♣Q♦J♠J♦, and the flop comes J♥3♣4♥.

22. When you are in a multiway pot and find yourself in one of these spots, how do you play?

Very cautiously.

Your Starting Hand

1. Except for the very best starting hands, what can happen to any hand that you hold?

It can be counterfeited by a similar starting hand either one notch higher or slightly lower with an additional draw.

2. How often does this happen?

Not every time, but a lot in multiway pots.

3. What does this mean?

You must be careful with many hands that look reasonably good.

4. What if you are in a short-handed pot?

You have to play these hands out.

5. Since most hands run very close, what is the most important skill?

The ability to outplay your opponent.

6. Why do low hands have a playing advantage over high hands?

Because scare cards often appear, and the holder of the high hand does not know what to do.

7. What is the disadvantage of the low hand?

The high hand can force the low hand to call all bets.

8. What do high hands, even those that have made big hands, frequently need in multiway pots?

Redraws.

9. If a third low card comes on the river, besides making a low, what else might it make?

A small straight that can beat a high set.

10. What if this low card also gives the high hand a flush?

Then it is not so bad.

11. Why is an ace a key card?

Because it is needed to make the nut low when there is no ace on board, it can make the nut flush, and when it makes a high straight, it is the nut straight.

12. If you play an ace and a lot of people take the flop, what does this mean?

It is likely not only that one or more of your opponents holds an ace, but also that someone has an ace-deuce or an ace-trey.

13. In general, what happens if you start with three or fewer coordinated cards?

Your hand will prove to be very costly.

14. What is the exception?

You hold an ace-deuce, which does not always require all four cards working together.

15. What might be another possible exception?

A hand like ace-trey-four-ten, with the ace suited to one of the other cards.

16. Why is it important to have all four cards working together?

Because many pots get jammed on the later streets, and you often need the extra outs.

Starting With Big Pairs

1. Comment on a hand that includes two aces.
   It is a key hand in Omaha eight-or-better. When your hand also includes a deuce, and to a lesser extent a trey, it is a premium hand.

2. What is the bad part of having two aces?
   When you make three of a kind, one of the cards needed to make a low is now on board.

3. What if you make a high set, such as three kings?
   It is not as likely that someone will share a low with you.

4. What if you have two aces without a good low card?
   You can't stand a lot of action before the flop, unless you are suited up or have four high cards.

5. How would you play A♠A♥10♦7♣?
   You would discard this hand if there is any kind of action early.

6. If there is a lot of action, what does it probably mean?
   Someone most likely holds an ace-deuce, and your chances of making three of a kind have diminished.

7. What about other big pairs?
   They do poorly unless the pot is short-handed, the flop comes with three high cards, or the pairs are joined by two other related high cards.

8. What happens as big cards get lower?
   Their value drops way off.

9. Why is that?

Because when you make a straight, it puts low cards on board.

10. Example?

A hand like 9♣9♦8♣8♠ is close to the worst four cards that you can be dealt.

When You Are First In

1. What does a call do?
   It tends to promote multiway pots.

2. When should you raise?
   When you are hoping to narrow the field to three or fewer players.

3. What if the game is loose?
   You can expect multiway pots whether you just call or raise.

4. How should you play in this situation?
   According to what best fits your style.

5. If the game is loose but there is a lot of raising, why might you just want to call?
   To see who does the raising so you can gauge the strengths of the various hands.

6. In a tight game, how should you usually bring it in?
   With a raise.

7. What are you hoping to accomplish with your raise?
   Either to steal the blinds or to play against only the blinds.

8. What typically happens if you don't bring it in with a raise?
   You often find yourself caught in the middle, even if the game is tight.

9. In general, should you raise a lot?

No. You should not raise unless the game is tight and you are confident that you can get in a heads-up confrontation.

10. What often happens when you are playing heads up?

You can win the high with very weak hands, plus you can bluff players out since most of your opponents will play for low.

How To Play Your Hand

1. If you decide to play your hand, what must you determine?
   Whether you want lots of opponents or a few opponents, a big pot or a small pot.

2. What should influence your decision?
   The type of players who are behind you, your position, the game, and even how you are doing in the game.

3. But what is your decision mainly based on?
   The strength of your hand.

4. Example?
   If you are raising and reraising, you usually should have the nuts, especially if you are on the low side.

5. What else should you consider?
   How easy it is for your hand to be counterfeited later on, or how easy it is for a scare card to come that may prevent an opponent from jamming.

6. If it is easy for you to get counterfeited, what precaution should you take?
   In this case, you might not want to give a lot of action until all the cards are out.

7. Suppose you have the high and you want the player with the probable low to jam it. However, your opponent might fear that if a small card comes on a later street, his hand can be ruined, or perhaps he may just be afraid to bet. What should you do?
   You usually should play fast.

8. Why is a little deception early good?

    Because many people will form an opinion about your hand and stick with it.

9. Give an example of deceptive play.

    On an early round, you occasionally do not raise in a spot where most other players will raise, or you will bet with a marginal hand.

10. What might this type of play do for you?

    Someone could misread your hand and give you lots of action with the second-best hand.

Play on the Flop

1. What should you do any time that an ace hits on the flop?
   Tighten up significantly.

2. What typically can happen if an ace hits the board with another low card?
   A player who waits for premium hands can have the nut low draw with a pair of aces and possibly other draws working.

3. Suppose the flop is Q♥10♣2♠, you hold two queens, and there is a fair amount of money already in the pot. What should you do?
   Raise or perhaps try for a check-raise in an effort to knock out other players.

4. Now suppose you have a big wrap-around straight draw with the same flop. Should you raise?
   No, as you do not want to knock out other players.

5. What if you think one of your opponents has a hand similar to your hand?
   You probably would want to eliminate all players with low draws.

6. What might this allow you to do?
   To split the high with no one getting the low, to win with just a high pair, or if low cards come, to bluff your opponent out.

When You
Have the Best Hand

1. What should you do when you believe you have the best hand?
   Either bet or raise, except possibly on the flop.

2. Why should you sometimes make the flop an exception?
   To see whether a scare card or a counterfeit card comes to knock you off.

3. Example?
   You have A♣2♦J♥Q♥, the flop is 5♣6♠7♦, and the pot is multiway. Since all you have is a low, you want to be extremely careful before you put a lot of money in the pot.

4. What do cautious players generally do when they have an ace-deuce low but do not have redraws?
   They almost never raise until all the cards are out.

5. What does this mean?
   If you are playing against a tight player, there is a possible nut low out, and he is in there calling, he usually has it.

6. Even though this approach works in the smaller games and in loose games at the higher limits, why does it fail in tight games?
   Because good players won't give tight players action.

Automatic Play

1. In a heads-up pot, suppose you flop two pair and it looks as though your opponent has a low draw. What should you do if a low card comes on the turn?

Check and call through the river.

2. If you flop what looks like the best hand, especially heads up, what should you do?

Punish your opponent.

3. What if your opponent has you beat?

He usually will play back. There is very little slow-playing in Omaha eight-or-better.

4. What if the pot is contested by many players?

Some of your opponents will slow-play a bit more.

High Versus Low
in Three-Handed Pots

1. Suppose you have a high hand that is not going to be easily beat, and it appears that both of your opponents have made good low hands or have good low draws. What should you do if one of the low hands bets and you are next?

In this situation, you should just call.

2. Why should you just call?

Since you are going to split the pot, just calling will enable you to chop up the player behind you.

3. Suppose your high hand is weak and there is some chance that it can be beat?

In this case, it may be correct to drive out the third player.

4. On the river in a three-handed pot, if a high hand bets, a low hand calls, and you are next with the nut low, should you automatically raise?

No, as you have to consider how the person in the middle plays.

5. If he is a weak player, what should you do?

Go ahead and jam it.

6. What if he is a fairly good player?

You probably should just call.

Loose Games

1. What type of hands do you need in loose games?
   Hands that can make the nuts with draws and redraws to even better hands.

2. What about just having an ace-deuce?
   It will split the low or get counterfeited too often.

3. Be specific about hands required in loose games.
   You want hands that have the best low, or the best low draw with chances to back-door flushes, regular nut flush draws, straight draws, or trips, or a wheel with a chance of a six- or seven-high straight.

4. Why does being suited add value to your hand?
   Because you often can jam when you make the low if you also have a draw at the high side.

5. What about the bigger hands, such as four high straight cards suited up?
   These hands don't do well in this type of game, unless the pot gets played short-handed or you can enter the pot cheaply.

6. Give some premium hands for loose games.
   A♠2♥4♠5♥, A♣K♦2♥3♣, A♥A♦3♥4♠, and A♠A♦2♣ (any card).

7. What about four small cards?
   They can do very well, but they almost always require an ace to hit on the flop. You usually want to get in cheap with this hand.

Multiway Versus
Short-Handed Play

1. In a multiway pot, you need a very good hand. What about in short-handed pots?

It doesn't matter as much.

2. What are the most important factors in short-handed pots?

Your position and playing against weaker opponents over whom you have good control.

3. Why are these factors important?

Because if a weak player can't make a low, he frequently folds, and unless he has a great high hand, he gets scared by any card that comes out.

4. What happens to typical players?

They become accustomed to seeing many cinches in multiway pots and thus don't realize that in heads-up pots, they are not running into monster hands all the time.

5. What does this mean?

You can bluff and maneuver your opponents when the pot is short-handed.

6. In a multiway pot, what does it mean when someone bets from an early position?

He usually has the nuts or something close to it.

7. How does this affect your play?

You usually should get out, unless you also have a big hand.

8. Suppose four or five players are in the pot and it is clear that they have fairly good hands. You have a wrap-around hand with draws at both a good low and a good high, but these draws are not for the nuts. What should you do?

In this situation, you usually should fold.

9. What if the pot is heads up and you hold the type of hand just described?

You can go ahead and jam.

10. Example?

You start with A♦3♣6♦9♣, and the flop comes 5♥7♣K♣. If many players are still in and it looks as though there may be a lot of action, you should fold. But if you are heads up and have a fairly big hand, you should play it as such, unless you are against a very tight player.

11. What about a hand like A♠2♦4♥J♠?

This hand does OK heads up. But because of the redraw possibilities, it does very well if you expect many players.

12. What is the best hand to have in a heads-up pot?

The high hand. But you also would like to have a low draw, even if it is a poor one.

13. Why do you also want a low draw?

Because you might be sharing the high hand with your opponent.

14. Suppose you have what looks like a big hand but there are many possibilities the other way?

You must plan for these possibilities and determine the best way to deal with them.

15. Example?

In a two-handed pot, you start with A♣K♠J♦10♠ and the flop is 9♥8♣7♦. Even though you have the nuts for high and no low is yet made, if your opponent plays back at you, you could be against the same high hand as you hold, plus a low draw. Consequently, you may want to check and call on fourth street, no matter what hits.

16. How do most people play when the game becomes five-handed or less?

Along the same lines as they normally play.

17. What does this mean?

You have the opportunity to steal a lot of blinds.

Scare Cards

1. What does it mean when a player who has been just calling suddenly starts betting or raising on the river?

> Either he had the nuts the whole way or he just made the best hand.

2. What should you do in this situation?

> You probably should go out, no matter how big the pot is. This is especially true if the last card could have made the nuts for either high or low.

3. Example?

> You start with K♦K♣Q♥Q♠. On fourth street, the board is K♣9♥5♠4♠, and the last card is the 8♠. If a player who has been just calling all along now bets, and the pot is subsequently raised by another player who isn't likely to be going low, you easily could be against the nut flush as well as the nut low.

4. Suppose the card that comes out is a scare card but not one that makes all the hands?

> In this case, you don't have to check and give up all the bets on the end.

5. Example?

> If the last card given in the previous example was the 8♣ instead of the 8♠, automatically throwing away your hand is wrong, even though someone may have made a straight with a seven-six.

6. How should you play in this spot?

A lot of times you should go ahead and bet. If you get raised or the action becomes strong against you, then you can give it up.

Getting Counterfeited

1. Do you get counterfeited frequently in Omaha eight-or-better?
   Yes.

2. Example?
   Suppose you hold A♠A♥4♦5♠ and the flop comes A♦2♣3♠. You have three aces, plus a wheel, which is the nut low. If there is a great deal of jamming on both the flop and fourth street, and a four or five hits on the river, you probably will be quartered by someone holding a six-high straight.

Getting Quartered

1. Even though you don't get many opportunities to make great plays in Omaha eight-or-better, when you have the chance to knock out someone who is drawing to the same hand that you are, should you try to do so?
   Yes.

2. What if you can't knock out this player?
   You should throw away your hand.

3. Example?
   If you hold just an ace-deuce and there is a lot of multiway action early, someone else also has an ace-deuce. Consequently, you probably should fold your hand.

4. What is the exception to folding?
   When you have other winning draws working in the hand.

5. Is it difficult to knock out someone who has an ace-deuce draw by raising into him?
   Yes.

6. But what if someone raises into you?
   You probably should get out.

7. What will typical players do?
   They will call the raise cold and then often find themselves quartered.

Playing Against Steamers

1. What effect do the tough beats in Omaha eight-or-better have on some players?

The beats turn some players into steamers.

2. How will the steamers play?

They will steam early in the hand.

3. What about late in the hand?

They usually won't be raising or putting a lot of action in the pot, because they are still aware that it is too easy to look at a cinch hand.

4. When someone is steaming, do you want to isolate him?

Not usually.

5. Why not?

Because in Omaha eight-or-better, what hurts a weak hand the most is having many players against it.

6. What will isolating an opponent do?

It will make his hand a lot closer in value to your hand.

7. When is this particularly true?

When you hold a hand that can stand multiway action.

8. What if you have strictly a high hand?

Then you might be better off trying to isolate the steamer.

9. Can you get into trouble in this spot?

Yes. In loose games, other players usually will call behind you.

Playing Against
Tight, Solid Players

1. What must you do in this game?
   Get a line on your opponents. You must observe the type of hands they play and how they play them.

2. What type of hands do some people play?
   Low hands, plus a few premium high hands.

3. How do you play against these players if only one low card comes on the flop?
   You frequently can either bluff them out or beat them with a weak high hand.

4. Is position important?
   Yes. Some players are very tight in early position but loosen up if they can come in late.

5. What is the best way to save money?
   Don't give any action to those players who play very tight and very solid.

6. What if the pot is large and one of these tight, solid players comes out betting or raising, or he is in there on a jammed hand?
   He almost always has the nuts for low and usually has some kind of nut draw for the high side.

7. What does this mean?
   It doesn't pay to stay in these pots.

8. How do you spot this type of player?

He is not in many pots, he does not raise very often, and he almost always shows the nuts on the end.

9. What advantage do you have against these players?

You usually will know where they stand.

10. Where do you want these players seated?

To your right.

11. Why?

Because you will know that when they enter the pot, you should go out with all but your very best hands.

12. What if three or four of these tight players happen to be sitting in a row?

You probably would prefer to have them across from you.

13. Why?

Because if they are situated directly on your right, you probably will find yourself playing many hands out of position with the looser players on your left.

14. What is another advantage to having tight, unimaginative players on your right?

As the game becomes short-handed, they won't adjust.

15. What will this enable you to do?

To play many hands against the blinds.

16. What about when you are in the blind?

Tight players will be in the attack position but will do very little stealing.

17. What if one of them raises?
    You won't have to defend, as he will have a premium hand.

18. What if the little blind just calls and he is a tight, solid player?
    You can raise and frequently outplay him.

19. What if a tight, solid player is on your left?
    You ordinarily could steal the blind from him.

20. What is the problem with this in Omaha eight-or-better?
    Unless the game is very tight, it seldom happens that you are on the button and no one else comes in.

Your Playing Style

1. If you are the type of player who prefers to play tight and who makes good laydowns, what should your strategy be?
   To just call most of the time.

2. What if you are playing in a game where a lot of the pots are raised early?
   Many of your laydowns will be wrong.

3. What if you are a player who usually knows where he stands?
   It doesn't hurt to build the pots and lock your opponents into their hands.

4. What if you tend to call too much?
   You are better off building the pots early. You also should try to call less.

5. What if you are a timid, passive player who wants to play only the nuts?
   You probably should push your hands more than you normally do.

6. What if you are a weak player who plays too loose and calls too much?
   You shouldn't be playing Omaha eight-or-better.

Reading Hands

1. What is the most common way to read hands?

Analyze the meaning of an opponent's check, bet, or raise, and then consider the plays he has made *throughout the hand*, along with the exposed cards, to come to a determination about his hand.

2. Is it a mistake to put an opponent on a hand early and to stick with your initial conclusion?

Yes.

3. Suppose that before the flop, an opponent calls after you raise. On the flop, two small cards appear, as well as two suited cards, and he raises after you bet. An offsuit eight hits on the turn, but when you check, he also checks. What is a likely hand for him?

A flush draw.

4. What if a flush card comes on the end?

You should not bet into your opponent.

5. What if the flush card does not hit on the river?

You might want to check and try to induce a bluff.

6. But what if you have only a low made and cannot beat a weak high?

You may want to bet, since there is a reasonable chance that you can pick up the whole pot.

7. In practice, what should you try to determine?

Whether your opponent has a bad hand, a mediocre hand, a good hand, or a great hand.

8. If an opponent bets on the end, what type of hand is he unlikely to have?

A mediocre hand.

9. What is a complementary way to read hands?

To work backward.

10. Suppose someone cold calls a raise and a reraise before the flop, and the flop comes A♠9♣J♦. The fourth-street card is the 6♥, and your opponent is able to raise on fourth street. What is his probable hand?

A set of aces. It does not seem possible that this player would have called on the flop if he had something like a three-card low or a big pair smaller than aces before the flop.

11. Suppose on fourth street that the board is J♦2♣7♠8♣. The pot is multiway, and a player who called the bet on the flop now raises. Does this person just have the nut low?

No, even though it is likely that he started with an ace-trey.

12. Why is that?

Since the pot is being contested multiway, he would be afraid that he might get quartered.

13. What about three of a kind?

He is unlikely to have trips, as he would not have raised when the straight card hit.

14. What does this player most likely have?

The nut low and a draw at the nut flush.

15. When you have reduced your opponent's possible hands to a limited number, what do you use to determine what he probably holds?

Mathematics.

16. Suppose an extremely loose and aggressive opponent just calls before the flop. Two high cards flop — which gives you top set — you bet and he calls. On fourth street, an ace hits, which could make a straight, and this player bets into you. What should you do?

Raise, as he probably has aces up.

17. Why is that?

Because he is not likely to have made three aces or he would have raised before the flop.

18. What if you get reraised, meaning that you probably are against a straight?

You have a lot of outs to improve.

19. What if your opponent is tighter and more conservative?

In this case, you should just call.

20. Suppose you start with A♣K♦10♥10♦. You raise, and an opponent behind you reraises. The flop comes king high. You check and your opponent bets. What should you do?

If you think your opponent is as likely to have a hand like ace-deuce-trey as he is to have a pair of aces, you should at least call.

21. What is your play if an ace hits on a later street and your opponent bets again?

Your play is to raise if you know this opponent would still bet if he had only two aces.

22. What is another factor in reading hands and deciding how to play your own hand?

The number of players in the pot.

23. How do players tend to play their hands in multiway pots?

Much more straightforwardly.

24. When else do they play in a more straightforward manner?
    When several players are yet to act.

Psychology

1. What is meant by "the psychology of poker"?

Getting into your opponents' heads, analyzing how they think, figuring out what they think you think, and even determining what they think you think they think.

2. If you try to steal before the flop and are reraised by a strong opponent who knows you would attempt to steal in this position, what may be the correct play for you?

To raise back and then to bet on fourth and fifth streets.

3. Would you make this play against a weak player?

No.

4. When an opponent bets in a situation where he is sure that you are going to call, is he bluffing?

No.

5. Example?

If you have been betting all the way, you bet again after all the cards are out, and a player raises you, he is not bluffing.

6. Do players generally raise as a bluff on fourth street?

No. However, tough players will raise on fourth street with a mediocre hand that has some potential to become a very strong hand.

7. When might your opponent be bluffing?

When there appears to be a good chance that you will fold.

8. Give an example.

   Suppose that no one bets on fourth street, a small pair and two high cards are on board, and another small card hits on the river. If one of your opponents now bets, and he is the type of player who would try to pick up the pot with nothing, it may be correct for you to call or raise with a weak hand.

9. In deciding whether to bet, what else is important to consider?

   What your opponent thinks you have.

10. If your opponent suspects a strong hand, what should you do?

    Bluff more.

11. Give an example.

    You raise on the flop, which shows two suited cards and only one small card, and a blank hits on fourth street. If you check on fourth street but bet again on the river when a third suited card lands, it is difficult for many of your opponents to call with less than a flush. So bet your weaker hands in this spot.

12. What if your opponent suspects that you are weak?

    Don't try to bluff, but bet your fair hands for value.

13. Example?

    If both you and your opponent checked on fourth street, you frequently can bet one big pair on the end for value.

14. Should you ever intentionally make an incorrect play?

    Yes.

15. Why?

    Because you are trying to affect the thinking of your opponents for future hands.

16. Give an example.

Before the flop, you occasionally can reraise a late-position player, who may be on a steal, when you hold something like deuce-trey for low and two face cards.

17. What kind of players do these types of plays work well against?

Players who are good enough to try to take advantage of their new-found knowledge, but who are not good enough to realize that you know this.

Questions and Answers

Afterthought

Again, these questions are not designed as a replacement for the material in the text. Their purpose is to help keep you sharp between full readings of *High-Low-Split Poker Omaha Eight-or-Better For Advanced Players*. I recommend that when you believe you have become a winning Omaha eight-or-better player that you reread the text material every other month and review the questions about once a week. Also, remember to cover the answers and to think through those questions that you have trouble with. In addition, attempt to relate the questions to recent hands that you have played, and try to determine which concepts were the correct ones to apply.

Another thing to keep in mind, as has been mentioned several times in this book, is that Omaha eight-or-better played at the higher limits is not simple. This means that you should be a student for life. It takes a long time to become an expert player, which is why continuous review of these questions (and the rest of the material in this book) is an absolute necessity.

Conclusion

An attempt was made to show that Omaha eight-or-better is really two games. At the lower limits, many players play poorly, and many players are frequently in each pot. Consequently, in a low-limit game, a tight, straightforward strategy usually will be successful, although there is still more to winning than just waiting for an ace-deuce.

But at the higher limits, where many expert players can be found and where most of the games are fairly tight, Omaha eight-or-better requires much skill. You must understand the differences between the hands; know the types of hands that your opponents like to play and how they like to play them; have a plan for how you want to play your hand, which may include a possible bluff; and be aware of the chances that your hand may get counterfeited or that you may get quartered. In addition, you need to know to whom you can give action and against whom you need to be very cautious.

Perhaps the least known advice given in this text has to do with bluffing in short-handed pots when high cards flop. In fact, I suspect that some readers will think bluffing is recommended too much in these situations. Rest assured that such is not the case. I know not only from a theoretical point of view, but also from much practical experience; that these plays are correct and they are part of a strong winning strategy.

This book should have a major impact on those of you who read and study it, as well as on the games themselves. In general, there will begin to be more tough players around, meaning that some games will be tougher to beat. I expect this text to be a significant contributor to the future growth of Omaha eight-or-better, making more games available so the expert player will have more games from which to choose. Consequently, the book should benefit those of you who make a commitment to studying the ideas that it contains.

Finally, serious players who ignore the contents of this book will simply be left behind. This is probably true even if you are currently having a successful run at the game. This should give you an idea of how strong I believe the strategies and concepts in *High-Low-Split Poker Omaha Eight-or-Better For Advanced Players* really are.

Glossary

Ante: A bet required from all players before the start of a hand.

Baby: A small card, specifically an ace, deuce, trey, four, or five.

Back-door flush (or straight): A player is said to have made a back-door flush when both of the last two cards make his flush, even though he may have played on the flop for some other reason (such as holding a pair or a four straight).

Bad beat: When a big hand is beaten by someone who makes a long-shot draw.

Bicycle: Ace, deuce, trey, four, five — the best possible low hand; also called a "wheel" and a "baby straight."

Blank: A card that comes on either fourth or fifth street and is obviously not of any value to any player's hand.

Blind: In Omaha eight-or-better, a forced bet that one or more players must make to start the action on the first round of betting. The blind rotates around the table with each new deal.

Bluff: A bet or raise with a hand that you do not think is the best hand.

Board: In Omaha eight-or-better, the five cards that are turned face up in the center of the table; in seven-card stud eight-or-better, the four cards that are dealt face up to each player.

Bring-in: In seven-card stud eight-or-better, the forced bet that the lowest card showing must make.

Button: In Omaha eight-or-better, a small disk that signifies the player who is in last position when there is a house dealer.

Call: To put in the pot an amount of money equal to an opponent's bet or raise.

Calling cold: Calling a bet and raise all at once, as opposed to being in for the original bet and then calling a raise.

Check: To decline to bet when it is your turn.

Check-raise: To check and then raise after an opponent bets.

Cinch: A hand that cannot lose in at least one direction.

Counterfeit: In Omaha eight-or-better, a board card that duplicates a card in your hand and thus negates the value of your hand.

Dead card: In stud games, a card that already has been seen.

Dog: A hand that is not the favorite to win the pot.

Door card: In seven-card stud eight-or-better, the first exposed card in a player's hand.

Drawing dead: Being in the position where the cards you are hoping to catch still will give you a losing hand.

Family pot: A pot in which most of the players at the table are involved.

Fifth street: In Omaha eight-or-better, the fourth and final round of betting on the last card; in seven-card stud eight-or-better, the third round of betting (on the third upcard).

Flop: In Omaha eight-or-better, the first three community cards, which are turned face up simultaneously and start the second round of betting.

Flush: Five cards of the same suit.

Forced bet: A required bet to start the action on the first round of betting in seven-card stud eight-or-better.

Fourth street: In Omaha eight-or-better, the fourth card on board and the third round of betting; in seven-card stud eight-or-better, the second round of betting (on the second upcard).

Freeroll: A situation where two players have the same hand but one player has a chance to make a better hand.

Gut shot: A draw to an inside straight.

Heads up: Playing against a single opponent.

Hog: To win the whole pot.

Hogger: A hand that wins the whole pot.

Implied odds: The ratio of the total amount of money you expect to win if you make your hand to the bet you must now call to continue in the hand.

Jam: To bet or raise with the intention of reraising if the action is not closed when it returns to you.

Kicker: A side card.

Limp in: To call a bet rather than to raise. (This usually applies only to the first round of betting.)

Live card: In stud games, a card that has not yet been seen and is therefore presumed likely to be still in play.

Lock: A hand that cannot lose in at least one direction.

Muck: To throw away your hand; also the dead cards in front of the dealer.

Multiway pot: A pot in which more than two players are involved.

Nuts: A cinch hand.

Offsuit: Cards of different suits; used to describe two-card combinations in Omaha eight-or-better and the first three cards in seven-card stud eight-or-better.

On the come: Drawing to a straight or flush.

Outs: The number of cards left in the deck that should produce the best hand.

Overcall: To call a bet after another player has called.

Overcard: A card that's higher than the rank of an opponent's probable pair.

Overpair: In Omaha eight-or-better, a wired pair that is higher than any card on board.

Play back: To raise when someone bets or raises into you.

Put him on: To guess an opponent's hand and play accordingly. To put someone on a pair of queens is to read him for a pair of queens.

Quarter: In Omaha eight-or-better, to win only one-fourth of the pot.

Rag: A card that is not of any value to a player's hand.

Raise: To bet an additional amount after someone else has bet.

Razz: Seven-card stud played for low.

River: In Omaha eight-or-better, the last round of betting (on the fifth-street card); in seven-card stud eight-or-better, the last round of betting (on the seventh card).

Running pair: In Omaha eight-or-better, fourth- and fifth-street cards of the same rank (but of a rank different from any of the other cards on board).

Rolled up: In seven-card stud eight-or-better, three of a kind on third street.

Rough: Refers to the quality of a low hand. The rougher the hand, the poorer it is. For example, 8♣7♦6♣4♥2♠ would be considered a rough eight.

Scoop: To win the whole pot.

Second pair (third pair): In Omaha eight-or-better, pairing the second (third) highest card on board.

Semibluff: To bet with a hand that is probably not the best hand but that has a reasonable chance of improving to the best hand.

Set: Three of a kind. (In Omaha eight-or-better, this usually means a pair in your hand and a matching card on board.)

Scare card: An upcard that looks as though it might have made a strong hand.

Side action: Regular poker games spread during the same time period that a poker tournament is held.

Sixth street: In seven-card stud eight-or-better, the fourth round of betting (on the sixth card).

Slow-play: To play a very strong hand as though it were a weak hand.

Smooth: Refers to the quality of a low hand. The smoother the hand, the better it is. For example, 8♣5♦4♣3♥A♠ would be considered a smooth eight.

Soft game: A poker game that contains several non-skilled players.

Steal: To cause your opponents to fold when you probably do not have the best hand.

Steam: To play badly because you are emotionally upset.

Straight: Five cards of mixed suits in sequence.

Suited: Cards of the same suit; used to describe two-card combinations in Omaha eight-or-better or the first three cards in seven-card stud eight-or-better.

Tell: A mannerism a player exhibits that may give away his hand.

Third street: In seven-card stud eight-or-better, the first round of betting (on the first three cards).

Top pair: In Omaha eight-or-better, pairing the highest card on board.

Turn: In Omaha eight-or-better, the fourth-street card.

Value bet: A bet on the end that should show a profit in the long run, even though it's not a sure thing.

Wheel: See bicycle.

Wired pair: In Omaha eight-or-better, a pair in hand; in seven-card stud eight-or-better, a hidden pair on the first three cards.

Index

NOTES

NOTES

NOTES